PAT GARRETT

and

BILLY THE KID

as I Knew Them

Frontispiece. John P. Meadows as a young man, from Charles A. Siringo's *The Song Companion of a Lone Star Cowboy; Old Favorite Cow-Camp Songs* (Norwood, Pa.: Norwood Editions, 1975 [1919]).

PAT GARRETT

and

BILLY THE KID

as I Knew Them

Reminiscences of
John P. Meadows

Edited by John P. Wilson

University of New Mexico Press
Albuquerque

© 2004 by the University of New Mexico Press
All rights reserved. Published 2004
Printed in the United States of America

10 09 08 07 06 05 04   1 2 3 4 5 6 7

Library of Congress Cataloging-in-Publication Data

Meadows, John P., 1854–1936.
Pat Garrett and Billy the Kid as I knew them :
reminiscences of John P. Meadows / edited by John P. Wilson.
    p. cm.
Includes bibliographical references and index.
ISBN 0-8263-3325-7 (cloth : alk. paper)
1. Billy, the Kid—Friends and associates.
2. Garrett, Pat F. (Pat Floyd), 1850–1908—Friends and associates.
3. Meadows, John P., 1854–1936.
4. Frontier and pioneer life—Southwest, New.
5. Outlaws—Southwest, New—Biography.
6. Sheriffs—Southwest, New—Biography.
7. Southwest, New—History—1848–
I. Wilson, John P. (John Philip), 1935– II. Title.
 F786.M493 2004
 363.2'092—dc22

                        2004011802

Design and composition by Maya Allen-Gallegos
Typeset in Century Light 10.5 / 13.2
Display type set in Mesquite, Birch, and Century Family

"I am not going to leave the country, and I am not going to reform, neither am I going to be taken alive again."

—*Billy the Kid to John P. Meadows, on the Peñasco, c. May 1–2, 1881 (quoted in* Roswell Daily Record, *February 16, 1931, page 6).*

Contents

List of Illustrations

Figures

Maps

Map 1. Arizona, New Mexico, and West Texas, with place names in John Meadows's reminiscences. Map courtesy of the author.

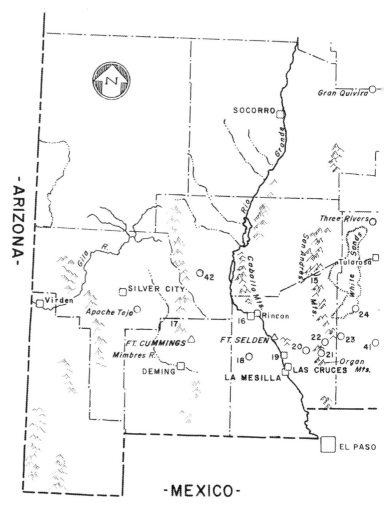

Map 2. Southern New Mexico, with places mentioned in John Meadows's reminiscences. Map courtesy of the author.

Place Names

1. Stinking Springs
2. C-Dot/Bar W Ranch
3. Carrizozo
4. Nogal Creek
5. Lincoln
6. Rio Bonito
7. Blackwater Creek
8. VV Ranch
9. Ruidoso (Dowlin's)
10. Rio Ruidoso
11. Mescalero
12. Blazer's Mill
13. Bent
14. Tularosa Creek
15. Hembrillo Canyon
16. Rodey (Colorado)
17. Cookes Peak
18. Mason's Ranch
19. Doña Ana
20. Organ

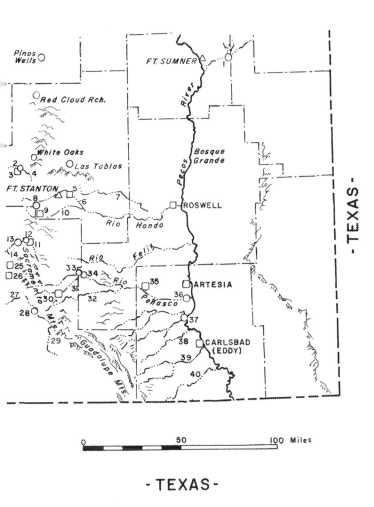

- TEXAS -

Acknowledgments

In 1985–86 Thomas Caperton and the New Mexico State Monuments division supported the research for my history of Lincoln, New Mexico, published in 1987. While engaged in this I came across John P. Meadows's reminiscences of "Billy the Kid As I Knew Him," a typed manuscript in the Philip J. Rasch files at Lincoln State Monument. I soon learned that some of Meadows's stories had appeared in the *Alamogordo News* in 1935 and 1936.

In 1996 I compiled and partially annotated Meadows's recollections. Apart from what he said in his own stories, his personal history was virtually unknown. He had not attracted attention from historians, and persons who remembered him had known him only casually or when they were children, more than sixty years earlier. The latter half of his life, from c. 1900 to 1936, had to be worked out from primary documents.

Dr. David Townsend of Alamogordo, New Mexico, introduced me to Mr. George Abbott, who as Otero County Treasurer in the 1930s recalled John Meadows as a nice-looking man who dressed well in Western style. Mrs. Norma Cinert and Lucille Marr had known him when they were children in Tularosa, New Mexico. They told me about his purchase of a whole block in downtown Tularosa (the Meadows Block), reportedly with money obtained from his second wife, a woman named Encarnación Gutiérrez, and that he lost this property in the 1930s, probably through a foreclosure. They recalled his serving as mayor of Tularosa, his reputation as a storyteller, and another wife in the 1920s.

My wife, Cheryl, found a letter by Meadows in an 1897 newspaper among New Mexico State University Library's Special Collections. This letter is included here as chapter 18. The Alamogordo Public Library staff made available their early Tularosa and Alamogordo newspaper microfilms. They also guided me to a local genealogist, Mrs. Jo Anderson, who told me the names of John Meadows's parents and first wife, and some personal details such as Charlie Siringo's dedication of *The Song Companion of a Lone Star Cowboy* to him. She had the information at hand because another researcher, name unknown or misplaced, had been inquiring about Meadows's family history. Mrs. Anderson regrettably passed away in February 2001.

In 1996 Mr. Abbott showed me how to use the books in the county clerk's office at the Otero County Courthouse. I built upon this knowledge during subsequent visits and also was allowed to examine the bound volumes of early Tularosa and Alamogordo newspapers on file there. I very much appreciate the assistance of both Mr. Abbott and the staff in the county clerk's office. Later I drove to Tularosa, where Village Clerk Margaret Gonzales allowed me to look through the Minute Book (#2) of the board of trustees, April 6, 1926, to December 2, 1936, and make notes. Meadows served as mayor of Tularosa from May 28, 1926, until May 3, 1928.

My biggest challenge lay in sorting out Meadows's marriages. From Mrs. Anderson I had learned the name and date of death of his first wife, Delia, who was buried at the cemetery in La Luz, New Mexico. When and where he married her I could not determine.

His second marriage, to Encarnación Gutiérrez, was recorded by an undated marriage certificate filed in the Otero County Clerk's office in 1901. The county clerks in Lincoln, Chaves, Eddy, and Doña Ana counties; the St. Francis de Paula parish registry office at Tularosa, the New Mexico State Records Center and Archives, and the Archdiocese of Santa Fe all lent their offices to confirming this marriage and to finding the dates of birth, baptism, and death for her, but without result. The Otero County Clerk's office had the death date, will, and probate file of yet a third wife, Mary (Tucker) Meadows. Eventually an obituary for her was found as well. Meadows had no children by any of his marriages.

Research for this volume, other than what I have acknowledged, is my own. Assembling the illustrations, on the other hand, has meant asking for aid from many others. Among the institutions that provided scanned photos on CDs or photographic prints are the Museum of New Mexico Photo Archives, the New Mexico State University Archives, the Historical Society for Southeast New Mexico, the Nina Stewart Haley Memorial Library, the University of New Mexico's Center for Southwest Research, and the New Mexico State Records Center and Archives. Several of these I visited repeatedly and Mr. Dennis Daily at the NMSU Archives and Mr. Arthur Olivas at the MNM Photo Archives were both patient and helpful in answering my requests. We didn't find everything I wanted, but photos of some persons and places may not exist.

The outstanding illustrations among all of these are the scanned and enhanced images of the young (undated) John Meadows; the Tularosa street scene c. 1903; and the 1915 interior of the Meadows Saloon in Tularosa. These and several others of Tularosa were generously provided by Mrs. Norma Cinert and the Tularosa Village Historical Society, with the enhancements done by Mr. Ken Riedlinger, the assistant editor, sports editor, and photographer of the *Tularosa Reporter.* For these, and to all of the agencies and individuals in Tularosa, Alamogordo, Las Cruces, Santa Fe, and elsewhere who helped to sort out the obscurities in John Meadows's life, it just suits me (as he might have said) to say thank you very much.

Finally, I have sought to comply with the suggestions offered by the manuscript's reader, Dr. Richard Melzer of the University of New Mexico at Valencia. One result has been to put the events in John Meadows's life into the larger context of his place and time. To some degree this has cast me as his biographer, which I had never intended. For turning one more of my manuscripts into a book, I am grateful to David V. Holtby, my editor at the University of New Mexico Press. And for her most excellent job of indexing this work, I thank Mrs. Dawn Santiago of Alamogordo, New Mexico.

Introduction

Cowboy, army guide, farmer, stock raiser, peace officer, and storyteller. John P. Meadows was all of these at one time or another in his eighty-two years, two-thirds of which he lived in New Mexico. His written legacy is one letter to a Las Cruces, New Mexico, newspaper and a second one at the Kansas State Historical Society, but as he reminisced about his life experiences, some listeners wrote these down. This book will make his stories available to everyone.

John Meadows began life on May 26, 1854, near Mechanicsville, Alabama, the son of M. P. Meadows and Maree Laurett of Georgia. His father was probably hospital steward Miles P. Meadows, who served with the Georgia 5th Infantry Regiment during the Civil War. The family included at least one sister as well. In the absence of family papers or any descendants, nothing is known of John Meadows's life from 1854 to 1873.[1]

At the age of nineteen he came to Texas to seek his fortune, arriving in Eastland County (between Fort Worth and Abilene) in the latter part of 1873. He worked off a loan from a cousin for his train and boat fares, then hired out as a camp helper to a buffalo hunter, driving teams to Fort Griffin and Big Spring. This and other experiences he related many years later, in a series of interviews. It is these reminiscences that allow us to follow his trail for the next twenty-five years, until he settled down in Tularosa, New Mexico.

From 1874 until March of 1880, Meadows lived a fiddle-footed life in Texas. A man named Joe Ruggles hired him to punch cows, and while working with this outfit Meadows taught himself how to write. Between 1874 and 1877 he helped herd cattle over various trails, from Fort Griffin and Fort Concho as far west as El Paso, north to Trinidad, Colorado, and Dodge City, Kansas. The livestock driven to Indian agencies at Fort Sill and

Fort Reno in present-day western Oklahoma were called commissary herds, issued as rations. These long drives in the peak years of the range cattle industry led him from Fort Stockton to Seven Rivers and Fort Sumner in New Mexico as well.[2]

In the winter of 1876–77, Meadows took up with Old Man Knox ("Uncle George" Knox) and hunted buffalo in the Fort Griffin country north of modern Abilene, Texas, until they "were about all gone," as he put it. Knox, whom he called "a mighty good man," was one of many frontier personalities John Meadows later characterized in his narratives. He worked for the Millet Brothers driving commissary herds from the Brazos country into Indian Territory (Oklahoma) and then bought a lot of Indian ponies that he took to Colorado. Much of this work brought him no money. Finally, he tried his hand at hunting wolves near Vernon, Texas. This turned hazardous when Comanche Indians raided the wolf hunters' camps.

Meadows's narrow escape when the Comanches chased him across an open prairie evidently turned his thoughts to a country he'd visited before—New Mexico. He had worked in cattle outfits with a young man named Tom Norris—"no better man ever lived"—and in the late winter of 1880 "he and me fixed it up to come to New Mexico." Meadows never looked back.[3]

John Meadows left no manuscripts, but he related these experiences and many others in interviews with one or more historians and in two serialized newspaper accounts. He was already seventy-six when this started, with the featuring of someone billed only as "Old Timer" in a historical pageant staged in Roswell, New Mexico. Its promoters termed this affair, *Days of Billy the Kid In Story, Song and Dance,* "one of the most unique and unusual entertainments ever attempted in this city." A sellout audience packed the junior high school auditorium for the performance on the evening of February 26, 1931. The *Roswell Daily Record* ran a series of short articles as teasers in the days before to publicize the event and its special guest.

All of this came about because members of the Chaves County Historical Society had taken serious exception to the 1930 MGM movie *Billy the Kid.* They determined that it should not go unchallenged and arranged for one of the few persons still living who knew both Billy the Kid and Pat Garrett to tell the public "the real facts" of the events of fifty years before.[4] When the evening came, more than one thousand people filled the auditorium to capacity. The program included the New Mexico Military Institute Band, square dancers, a fiddlers' contest, and a new song, "My Pecos Valley Home," composed and sung by Miss Elizabeth Garrett, daughter of former Sheriff Pat F. Garrett. It was a community affair and many of the persons involved—Hiram Dow, C. D. Bonney, Lucius Dills, Frank Coe—are prominent in Roswell and Pecos Valley history. Conspicuously absent is any reference to Maurice G. Fulton, the well-known Lincoln County War historian who lived in Roswell.[5]

Whether prompted by the onstage setting of cowboys around a campfire or something less tangible, the "Old-Timer," now revealed as John P. Meadows of Tularosa, gave a stellar performance. From time to time a person called "Cowboy," actually C. D. Bonney, would pose a question, starting off with "Tell us all about it, about Billy the Kid." The audience was not disappointed; Meadows spoke easily and his voice carried throughout the hall.[6]

Best of all, someone had arranged for a stenographic record. Revised and added to by Meadows, the Roswell newspaper published this in three long articles, in its issues for March 2, 3, and 4, 1931. To judge from the articles, the original narration must have taken hours, but it was well organized, coherent, and quite detailed; Meadows obviously held his audience and spoke without repeating himself. Some of these remarks were not repeated elsewhere; the references to Secundo and the Lapoint Saloon in Las Cruces, New Mexico, are found only in the March 2 article. With the exception of his comments about Billy Wilson, now known to be in error, his recollections that evening are highly creditable. Frazier Hunt, apparently the only author to cite these, included extracts from the Roswell newspaper articles in his 1956 book.[7]

Hunt used the Maurice G. Fulton Collection, which includes photocopies of the March 2 and 3, 1931, *Roswell*

Daily Record articles. Differences in phrasing and contents show that these were not the source of a typed transcript of Meadows's reminiscences, found in the Philip J. Rasch files at Lincoln State Monument in Lincoln, New Mexico. This seventy-eight-page manuscript, with an approximate date of 1931, has three main parts: "Cowboy in Texas," "Overland to California," and "Billy the Kid as I Knew Him." Nothing is known about the circumstances that led to its creation, nor do we know whether the titles were Meadows's own or Fulton's.

The February 26 "entertainment" in Roswell obviously caught the attention of Texas historian J. Evetts Haley. He interviewed Meadows on four occasions: at Tularosa in 1931 and 1933 and twice at Alamogordo in June of 1936. The Haley interviews have not been examined; the name index to these suggests that they are similar to what is given in the present volume. T. Dudley Cramer cited the Haley Collection as his reference for the Beckwith episode (see chapter 7).[8]

As a fourth source, the *Alamogordo News* printed at least thirty-nine articles "as told by John P. Meadows," all titled individually apart from a six-part series with the heading "My Personal Recollections of 'Billy the Kid'." The articles began on August 8, 1935, and continued through June 25, 1936. The one in the June 25 paper concluded with "(THE END)," as if Meadows intended to stop his reminiscences at that point, with Billy the Kid's escape from the Lincoln County Courthouse. In any event, John Meadows died at Alamogordo on June 23, 1936.[9]

The old cowboy's recollections tell nearly all of what we know about his life, from the time he and Tom Norris rode into Fort Sumner in March of 1880 until the late 1890s. He lived at any number of places around southeastern New Mexico while he worked for cattle ranchers, tried farming on his own account, turned to freighting, found employment with the Mescalero Apache agency, then at Eddy, New Mexico, and served as a deputy under Doña Ana County Sheriff Pat Garrett. In 1899 he settled at Tularosa and made it his home until 1933, when he moved to Alamogordo.[10]

My Personal Recollections of "Billy The Kid"

As Told By John P. Meadows, To A Representative Of The Alamogordo News

I have been asked by a number of people recently to relate reminiscences of my association with "Billy the Kid." I will begin and tell how I ran across him. As time goes on William Bonney, or "Billy the Kid," seems to be rated as one of the interesting characters of the old Southwest. And to tell the truth to many when in life he had quite a little personal charm to his friends.

At no time was I a member of his or any other gang. However, I had a few business dealings with Billy and he always treated me fairly. As we go along I will indicate that the man who is generally chronicled as having turned outlaw, really had some excellent traits along with some of his bad ones.

My first meeting with the Kid dates from a day or so after I came to New Mexico to stay, in the early days of 1880. I have told you that I was through the Fort Sumner country with cattle drives in the middle 70's. My partner, Tom Norris, and I were coming into Fort Sumner from the Vernon, Texas country. We had reached the edge of Fort Sumner, which was a little hamlet at that time. I was lying on the ground, under the shade of a large cottonwood tree, and was ill. The wind had taken my hat away beyond recovery three days before we reached Fort Sumner. I was waiting for Tom to go into the little town and get me a hat.

While I was lying there a fellow came along and gave me a sharp tap on the foot with the toe of his boot and said, "Old pardner, it looks like you are up against it." He told me to get up and go to his room. I told him that I could not go to anyone's room as I had too much vermin on me and that I had been out in the open for a long time.

He said to never mind about that. I have had millions on me; as for a hat, I'll go and get you one. He rolled up my bedding himself and carried it into his room and put it on an iron cot. He also gave me a hat which was a very good one. Where he got it I never knew.

Very soon Tom Norris came back. He said, "John, I can't find a hat in the town and there is no store here." I said for him to never mind the hat, "this young man (at that time I had never heard of any such man as William Bonney or 'Billy the Kid'), has found a hat for me.

I stayed in Bill's room for several days. This was in the Maxwell house. Billy and good old Mrs Maxwell (Pete Maxwell's mother), doctored my sun-burned face with sweet cream. The kid was around the place for several days and each day came to see that I had something to eat and that my face was doctored.

I soon got up and was able to get around. In the meantime Billy the Kid was dealing monte for Pete Maxwell's sheep herders and sheep shearers. This was his game and he was a master at the art of dealing monte. The kid had acquired 42 head of cattle that he won in these games. At this time he was on his good behavior and the officers were not molesting him. He made a proposition for me to take these cattle out to the vicinity where Portales is now. I agreed, and will tell you about the venture next week.

Fig. 1. John Meadows's first article about Billy the Kid, in the *Alamogordo News*, April 16, 1936.

By 1935, when the *Alamogordo News* began publishing the stories he related to their reporter, he could have been polishing some of these for up to fifty years. This may explain why there is so little variation when we have multiple versions. Aside from what the articles reveal, details about Meadows's life in New Mexico (and briefly in Arizona) are hard to come by. The 1880 Census in San Miguel and Lincoln counties, taken during June, did not include John Meadows although Thos. Norris dwelt in Roswell at the time, listed as a stage driver. Early in 1883, the Las Cruces newspaper interviewed John P. Gray of Tularosa about the unsolved murders of the Nesmith family (see chapter 10). Meadows was using the alias of Gray at this time, as he explains in chapter 12. He did not appear under the name Meadows or Gray in the 1885 Territorial Census.[11]

By the summer of 1885 he had resumed calling himself Meadows, but the Lincoln *Golden Era* gave a hint of what was to come with its reference to his storytelling:

> John Meadows, one of the liveliest boys in the country, was telling big yarns to the boys Monday. John says he went to Kansas City one time with nearly $500 and only stayed three days. At the end of that time he didn't have a cent, but as he said, "I had three or four car loads of experience."[12]

In one story that he dated to January 1892 (chapter 15) he first mentioned his wife, stepdaughter, and brother-in-law Mel Lusk. Although he neglected to give his wife's name, she was Cordelia Lusk Sikes, known as Delia, born in North Carolina in 1853. Delia had divorced her first husband, John R. Sikes Jr., the date not known. When or where she married Meadows is also unknown; careful searches of the Lincoln, Doña Ana, Eddy, and Chaves County records; the marriage records compiled by the Eddy County Genealogical Society in their journal *Pecos Trails;* and other sources yielded no information. Perhaps an itinerant minister married them and failed to file a record of their union. Delia's daughter, Callie Sikes, married Walter Trimble at Weed, New Mexico on December 22, 1892.[13] John Meadows obviously felt affection for his wife because his obituaries confirm that he was laid to rest alongside her in the cemetery at La Luz, New Mexico, where her gravestone now stands. She died June 17, 1893; no will or probate file is on record for her.

Although his silence about women was typical for the time, John Meadows might have told us much more when instead he remained quiet. One instance is his own role in the efforts to solve one of New Mexico's highest-profile murder cases—the presumed murders of Colonel Albert Jennings Fountain and his young son at Chalk Hill on February 1, 1896. More than two years passed before the arrests and preliminary hearing for William Carr and William McNew, both charged with the Fountain murders. At the hearing, Meadows testified that

Major W. H. H. Llewellyn had employed him during the search that followed Fountain's disappearance. It may have been Meadows who found the pool of blood near where the Fountains' buckboard left the road.[14] Territorial Governor W. T. Thornton quickly hired Pat Garrett to work on the Fountain case as a private investigator. Before the end of March (1896) he became chief deputy, and then acting sheriff of Doña Ana County. He assigned E. E. Banner and James Brent as deputies almost immediately, and Meadows's angry letter of March 10, 1897, tells us that Garrett had sent him and Brent to search for the bodies of Colonel Fountain and his son by August 1, 1896.[15]

Occasional newspaper references to Meadows show that he continued as a deputy sheriff through 1897 and 1898.[16] On April 3, 1898, the same day that Sheriff Garrett arrested Carr and McNew, he sent Deputy Meadows and a posse to the Jarillas and Sacramentos with warrants for Oliver Lee and James Gililland, charging them with the murders of Fountain and his son Henry. This was the posse that followed Lee to his ranch in Dog Canyon, but backed off and returned to Las Cruces when one of his gunmen told them that Lee was not at home![17]

Pat Garrett bided his time, until on July 10, 1898, two of his deputies rode into his own ranch, some ten miles north of the Cox ranch, with the news that Lee and Gililland would spend the night at Wildy Well. Garrett promptly set off with four deputies to make an attempted arrest that turned into a famous gun battle instead, with one deputy left dying. Meadows missed this because, as the *Rio Grande Republican* reported a week before, his foot had recently been wounded by an accidental revolver shot. It was slowly improving and he could walk with the aid of a crutch.[18]

The creation of Otero County early in 1899 put the site of the Fountain killings beyond Pat Garrett's jurisdiction, by a little less than one mile. After some complex maneuvering, Lee and Gililland came in and surrendered to Judge Frank Parker in Las Cruces. Their trial was held at Hillsboro in Sierra County, a more neutral location. It opened on May 25, 1899, and ran for eighteen days, during which Meadows was called to testify about the pool of blood. His cross examination revealed that he had once lived under the name of John Gray, and with this the questioning took an entirely new direction in an obvious attempt to discredit the witness:

Defense attorney Albert Fall: "Are you the same John Gray who was indicted in Smith county, Texas, for assault to commit murder, and sent to the penitentiary for two years?"

Meadows began to squirm, grow restless and get red in the face, until he finally turned to the judge and said he claimed the right to explain, if he had to answer all these questions. Fall probably smiled, confident that "he had hit the bull's eye" as one report put it.

The court assented, and Meadows blurted out: "No, I'm not the same man and never was there! I don't know nothing about that place." The courtroom went into an uproar and the tables were abruptly turned on Meadows's inquisitor. If Fall was not simply fishing, he may have been acting on information about someone else named John Gray, or perhaps he had picked up a whiff of the difficulties that Meadows explains here in chapter 12. In any case there was nothing to it, and perhaps to drive this home, the prosecuting attorney asked him to explain how he came by the name John Gray. Meadows did so, in his own unique way:

> It just about suits me to tell that. When I was nothin' but a boy I worked for John Sellman [Selman] and John Lawrence up about Fort Griffin. I knew them both to be murderers and thieves, but I was nothin' but a boy and had no sense. People advised me to cut loose from them and I left. The next year people livin' there took old Lawrence out and killed him and Sellman was afterwards killed by Geo. Scarborough at El Paso.
>
> Some time ago while fishing with Tom Norris, Billy the Kid and some other fellows, some men came along and happened to ask what my name was and Norris told them it was John Gray. That's how I came by that handle. I sailed under it five years.

One newspaper account said the lawyers, spectators, prisoners, and even the judge "joined in the laughter created by the droll story of the witness," and a reporter remarked that this was the most hilarious murder trial he ever attended. Even Pat Garrett must have smiled. When the jury received the case, it deliberated a whole eight minutes before declaring the defendants "Not Guilty." Now the courtroom dissolved in pandemonium.[19]

In his own mind, Meadows must have had good reasons for keeping silent about all of this in his reminiscences. He continued as a deputy sheriff at least through December of 1898, when another newspaper article, this one unfortunately damaged, hints at a more successful ending to a shoot-'em-up at La Luz, at that time still in Doña Ana County:

> The six-shooter, hip hurrah element, undertook to run a "blazer" over Deputy Sheriffs Meadows and Wilson, at La Luz, the other night. The battle stood ten to two, . . . deputies came out victori- . . . fellows came out. . . . amento.[20]

By next spring his days as a lawman had evidently ended; the Las Cruces paper noted that John Meadows came down from Tularosa the previous day and would leave tomorrow for Silver City.[21]

Perhaps Meadows moved to Tularosa in expectation of getting married again. The lady who soon became his second wife, Encarnación Gutiérrez, is elusive. She was born Encarnación Patron in March 1859, almost certainly a younger sister of Juan Patron of Lincoln County War fame. She married Joe Rafael Gutiérrez on December 6, 1873; the only marriage at this period recorded in the Catholic register for Santa Rita Parish in Lincoln County.[22] As a fourteen-year-old bride, she had a very traumatic introduction to married life. It would have been her wedding *baile* at Lincoln that the Horrell brothers shot up on the night of December 20, 1873, in a notorious incident of Lincoln

9

County's Horrell War. Her father, Isidro, and three other persons died in the gunfire.[23]

Oral tradition in Tularosa has it that Rafael or Ralph Gutiérrez became a gold miner and he supposedly left Encarnación with a lot of money. By 1895 she was a widow and had begun buying properties in Tularosa. Then in Book 1, Otero County Marriages, we find recorded her marriage to John P. Meadows by the parish priest at Tularosa, Father Migeon. However, the certificate filed for record on May 18, 1901, gave her name as Encarnación Patron and left the date of this marriage blank. The 1900 census schedule for Tularosa did list John Meadows with wife Encarnación, married one year, living with two of her six children. The St. Francis de Paula parish registry office in Tularosa has no record of Encarnación Patron, Gutiérrez, or Meadows, from 1869 to 1947. Neither does the New Mexico Bureau of Vital Records.[24]

What became of her is not known. In 1931 Meadows filed a sworn statement, probably to clear a property title, that said Encarnación P. Meadows was his lawful wife on March 11, 1905. By the 1910 Census, Meadows had no one living with him at La Luz and listed himself as a general farmer.[25] Presumably she died sometime between 1905 and 1910, but none of the surviving newspapers yielded a death notice. No will or estate probate is on file for her in Otero County. Nor did my search of Otero County deed records determine what became of her property holdings in Tularosa. These could have passed to her children, although the 1931 declaration indicates that her husband may have held some interest. Both owned lots in Block 34 of downtown Tularosa, but they bought these at different times, Encarnación in 1895 and John Meadows in 1914.

"Seldom-seen" might apply to Meadows himself before 1914. The *Alamogordo News* noted that he visited Alamogordo from Tularosa on June 27, 1900. Early in 1904 *The Tularosa Democrat* twice reported John Meadows in town from his sheep ranch near Salina[s] peak, the sheep there doing well. Salinas Peak now lies on White Sands Missile Range, west of Three Rivers, New Mexico. Three years later one of the Alamogordo newspapers carried an item about Meadows

Fig. 2. Meadows Saloon, Tularosa, February 5, 1915. Left to right: John
    Meadows, Jack Maxwell, Elija Cooper, Arthur Chalk, Jack Carnett,
    Geo. Rud, Nick Peck. Courtesy of Mrs. Norma E. Cinert and the
    Tularosa Village Historical Society.

having returned recently from Carrizozo, where he had been
employed by the Bar W cattle company.[26] The Bar W was the
Carrizozo Land and Cattle Company, one of the largest ranches
in the area and managed until 1912 by William C. McDonald,
New Mexico's first statehood governor.[27]

By 1910, as we saw above, John Meadows lived alone in
La Luz. Whatever his earlier circumstances, he became a sub-
stantial landowner in Tularosa beginning in 1914, when he
acquired most of what had been the Coghlan block (Block 33)
downtown and followed this with at least five additional pur-
chases, culminating with a release of mortgage in 1925 on his
original property. The price for the four lots bought in 1914
was $3,800 and he would have needed financial standing to
warrant receiving a mortgage to buy these.[28]

The local suspicion is that he was using Encarnación's
money, and this may be justified. He assumed the mortgage

on one other parcel and bought most of the remaining ones for "one dollar and other valuable considerations," which might mean anything. In the 1920 census he gave his occupation as real estate agent and was shown as the head or owner of household #96, followed in the schedule by nine "Renters." This accords with the recollections of Mrs. Lucille Marr and Norma Cinert of Tularosa that Meadows was the landlord of the Meadows block and rented out the buildings. He checked "widowed" as his marital status.[29]

The former range-rider had turned sixty-six (he said sixty-five) by the time of the 1920 census. He finally had a comfortable status in life and what appeared to be a solid retirement. From 1912 into 1916 he operated a bar or saloon, evidently in rented quarters (Block 32, Lot B). This cost him $400.50 a year for a liquor license.[30] The last year he was convicted of selling liquor to a minor and fined $25, with a ninety-day suspended sentence. Six months later he bought Lots 13 and 14 in Block 30 of West Tularosa for one dollar and the other considerations that became his stock offer.[31]

At the age of seventy-one John P. Meadows married a third time, to Mary Gordon Tucker, another widow. She had been married twice before, most recently to Tom Tucker until his death in 1920. According to historians W. A. Keleher and A. M. Gibson, Tom Tucker was a murderous gunman who came into New Mexico in the 1880s, fleeing homicide indictments in Arizona and Texas. He became part of the inner circle surrounding rancher Oliver Lee. A decade or so later, Sheriff Pat Garrett did his best to see Lee convicted for the Fountain murders. Meadows admired Garrett but at no time did he mention Lee or any of the parties around him. Mary Tucker married John Meadows on September 8, 1925, in Alamogordo, a curious alliance in view of her former husband's close association with Lee. Perhaps by 1925 the old antagonisms had mellowed.[32]

Tularosa's board of trustees called the now-retired Meadows to a new civil office when they voted unanimously on May 27, 1926, to appoint him mayor of the village, to succeed a mayor who had resigned. His term began well enough, with the board approving a franchise to furnish electric current to

Fig. 3. Tularosa, N.Mex., about 1903; view probably along Granado
Street. Photo courtesy of Tularosa Village Historical Society.

the town and the next year paying forty-six of its citizens from
one dollar to eighteen dollars each for labor on the streets.
After this public works program, nothing remarkable seems to
have happened. Mayor Meadows signed the minutes of the
meetings and at the next regular municipal election on April 3,
1928, he ran for office and lost.[33]

The Depression years had a serious and very negative
impact on John and Mary Meadows. Her obituaries indicate
that she had been ill for more than a year when she died on
February 2, 1933. She did leave a will and a probate file
(#533), in which her husband received her only possession,
a house and lot in Alamogordo. Just a year before her death
they mortgaged their principal property, three lots in downtown Tularosa, for $7,500 and signed a promissory note that
bore an annual interest rate of 10 percent. This was due in
six months and they probably never expected to pay it off. In
August of 1933 the lots were sold at auction to satisfy the note
and accumulated interest.[34]

The decline in John Meadows's own health is probably what
decided him to deed the house and property in Mary's will to

his nephew's wife, Leona Dunson, just eleven days after Mary's death.[35] Meadows then moved to Alamogordo and lived with his nephew and his nephew's wife. Perhaps too it was the combination of financial reverses and his own failing health that led him to extend the reminiscences he began in 1931 and 1933 into the more extensive series that the *Alamogordo News* published in 1935–36. These continued right up to the time of his passing. His death on June 23, 1936, prompted the local papers to give him a final tribute with their generous obituaries, reflecting "Uncle John's . . . long, varied and withal interesting life experiences," as one paper put it. Eleven years earlier, historian Charles Coan offered a neutral assessment that "He had broad and diversified frontier experiences, and his life has been one of activity and worthy achievement."[36]

Even after his death and burial, misfortune followed the old cowboy. For failure to pay his taxes in 1934, Lots 13 and 14 in Block 30 at Tularosa were deeded to the State of New Mexico, the tax deed record being dated February 1, 1938. The total sum of this default was forty-eight cents.[37] These lots must have been the last thing that he owned; he had no will or probate file. The heritage that he did leave has a historical value that we cannot measure in dollars.

The version of recollections and reminiscences "As Told By John P. Meadows to a Representative of the *Alamogordo News*" falls into two principal parts: his experiences in Texas during the 1870s, and his activities during the 1880s and '90s in New Mexico and, briefly, in Arizona. The dozen or so articles in which he described cattle drives and buffalo-hunting in west Texas were summarized earlier in this introduction. These accounts were a separate part of his life and would require an introduction of their own. Meadows indicated as much by telling all of them in 1935, while he largely related his New Mexico experiences in 1936 issues of the paper.

Several articles are omitted because they relate to episodes outside of his personal knowledge that date long before John Meadows came to New Mexico Territory, or they are largely speculative. These include the alleged discovery of Carlsbad Caverns in 1854, the 1868 Battle of Round Mountain, a frontier character named Cherokee Bill (Bill Kellum; not the notorious Cherokee Bill from Indian Territory), and his observations on the prehistoric population of Otero County.[38]

The other main source of Meadows's reminiscences is the photocopy of the typed transcript that may predate the Alamogordo newspaper articles by four to five years. This copy was in one of the three filing cabinet drawers of the Philip J. Rasch Collection, loaned to me in 1985 by the New Mexico State Monuments division while I was researching for what became *Merchants, Guns, and Money*. Everything loaned was returned to that collection, with copies of selected items made for reference use later. Although the typescript appears to be Fulton's own typing, the original is not in the Maurice G. Fulton Collections at the University of Arizona Library. Where and how Rasch obtained this copy, I have no idea. This manuscript is given a date of c. 1931 largely because of an internal reference to Billy the Kid's death fifty years before (chapter 1).[39]

Finally, something should be said about how these stories were edited for publication. They are a mosaic of his experiences, arranged here in the approximate chronological order of their happening. Every word not in square brackets [ ] is John Meadows's own. With respect to chapters 1 through 3, primary reliance is placed upon the typed transcript because it has better continuity and slightly more creditable dialogue. Numerous extracts from the parallel versions in the *Alamogordo News* and *Roswell Daily Record* are inserted to make the stories more complete and to add details. Almost nowhere does Meadows contradict himself between the newspaper and typescript versions, and when this does happen it is usually in a detail such as whether Pat Coghlan had forty-two or forty-three indictments against him. To articulate sentences, phrases, and paragraphs was usually not complicated, as the appropriate insertion points were obvious. The result is a much fuller narrative.

The spellings of names are given as found in the articles and transcript, although Pierce, not Pearce, is the usual spelling of that name (chapters 2 and 4). Similarly, the names

Cookes Peak, Cookes Range, and Cookes Canyon for the mountains and canyon near Fort Cummings (chapters 4 and 5) have officially replaced the older name of Cook's.

No stories were shortened in editing, but because the last dozen pages in the 1931 transcript are dissociated story fragments, a few of these that dealt with other topics had to be omitted. Meadows occasionally leaped ahead in time or reverted back to another story, which meant that sections sometimes needed to be rearranged to keep events in proper chronological order. He may sometimes have projected himself into situations where he had had only a peripheral role, and it seems clear that not always did he tell everything he knew about an episode. Where more is known or, as with Rito Montoya, Meadows may have confused his demise with someone else's, additions or corrections are given in the endnotes and epilogue. When we consider that apart from the single letter, everything we have by him is someone's transcription of Meadows's narrations, it's understandable that with the lesser-known events he stuck to the essentials in order to keep the story going. Apart from the events in Texas before 1880, nothing of significance has been omitted.

When I first read John Meadows's reminiscences in 1985, they reminded me of Colonel Jack Potter's stories, from about the same period but set farther north in eastern New Mexico.[40] I liked Potter's stories and still like the comparison, perhaps because both derive from the lively interest the two narrators had in their surroundings. While Meadows told mostly about unusual and interesting events, Potter focused more on personalities. On the other hand, the former deputy probably characterized Sheriff Pat Garrett better than anyone else with direct experience. Apart from John Meadows's Billy the Kid stories, neither emphasized the best-known or most dramatic happenings and individuals with whom they crossed paths.

One trail driver and writer called Jack Potter "the most cheerful liar west of the Mississippi."[41] This was ungenerous because it implied that he intended to deceive, when his purpose was only entertainment. Likewise, Meadows never

1111111

attempted to deceive anyone and his errors or discrepancies were honest mistakes, failures of memory. When he told something outside of his personal experience he often qualified it by saying, for example, "Poe and McKinney both told me the same thing."[42] As with Potter, I believe that Meadows's stories should be read as reminiscences by one who lived life on the frontier, and not faulted if they sometimes fail to meet historical expectations.

Another deputy sheriff wrote of his experiences in New Mexico. Dee Harkey, born in Texas in 1866, came to New Mexico in 1890 and as he says, was a peace officer in Eddy County from 1893 until 1911.[43] He arrived too late to find the vivid characters and unbridled lawlessness that might have backdropped his career in an earlier day. Harkey made the best of it by recounting the incidents he experienced as a law officer, and although he visited Las Cruces, La Luz, Tularosa, and Three Rivers he did not mention Meadows. The Eddy County deputy claimed to have written his book himself, but the hand of an editor is evident, and he lacked Meadows's storytelling abilities. Harkey's accounts are not always reliable, and an undated clipping from the *El Paso Times* pasted in the late Lee Myers's copy of *Mean as Hell* reported a district court decision whereby Harkey was required to publish a retraction of what he wrote about a Mr. Christmas as it was libelous. Lee Myers, an avid historian who lived in Carlsbad, New Mexico, for many years, found Dee Harkey less than creditable.[44]

Another near-contemporary of John Meadows who was a skilled writer as well drew upon her experiences in the closing days of the frontier in western New Mexico. Agnes Morley Cleaveland peopled *No Life for a Lady* with occasional references to Maynard Dixon, Eugene Manlove Rhodes, and Montague Stevens, all well known at the time, but the bulk of her stories involved incidents and persons that would be unknown but for her writings, which are believable as well as entertaining, and focused much more upon ranch life. Hers was actually a comfortable existence; Meadows's life was filled with uncertainty, such that daily living for him was sometimes hazardous and occasionally life-threatening. Meadows never mentioned meeting a writer, although he must have known Gene Rhodes, and he may well have met Emerson Hough. If he did, they could readily have seen him as "source material" whose life had "dramatic value," much as Cleaveland came to realize this from her encounter with a lady author in search of local color.[45]

Meadows had all of this that anyone could wish for. His were not cowboy stories, but he would probably have laughed long at Cleaveland's anecdote where a cowboy had laughed uproariously at a visitor's distaste for sleeping in a bed infested with "soogins":

> "You should laugh," retorted the visitor. "I happen to know that you slumber in your bed."
> The cowboy turned purple. "No man can say that about me and git off with it," he roared.
> The Morleys rescued the visitor.[46]

According to Loraine Lavender, Agnes Morley Cleaveland's daughter, when people asked her mother if something really took place the way she described it in *No Life for a Lady,* her reply would be: "Well, it could have happened that way."[47]

Meadows commented that Pat Garrett had a dry wit, and the same can occasionally be seen in his own use of language. The episodes are still humorous when he does this because you don't see them coming. Sharing a sense of humor is probably one reason why John Meadows and Pat Garrett got along well in their twenty-two years of association. What underlay their eventual separation, if anything more than Meadows settling in Tularosa with his second wife, we are not told. Despite his claim near the end of chapter 3, he could not have served more than about two and one-half years as a deputy under Garrett, and chapter 17 suggests that his service may not have been continuous. This same long-term attachment to Pat Garrett is also evident with John Poe and Jim Brent.

Southeastern New Mexico in the 1880s and 1890s: The Context of John Meadows's Reminiscences

One historian called her history of southeastern New Mexico *Forgotten Frontier,* while another subtitled his account of the Tularosa country *Last of the Frontier West.*[48] Perhaps both had recognized that what unifies the Tularosa Basin and the mountain ranges to the east of it is their relative isolation from the rest of New Mexico. This physical, and economic, separation initially helped to make possible the climactic historical event there, the Lincoln County War of 1878–1879. After that, the old ways pretty much continued, although with a few important changes.

Before 1880, the only way to make a living in the Tularosa country outside of the original farming settlements at Lincoln (settled in 1855), Tularosa (1862), and La Luz (1865?) was to claim land in the mountain valleys and try to establish a small farm or ranch, hoping to exchange your produce for credit with local merchants; or go to work for one of the few ranchers large enough to employ people (such as John Chisum along the Pecos or Pat Coghlan at Tularosa). The merchants in turn hoped to monopolize trade with the army and Indian agencies, which were practically the only entities that paid money. There was also the extralegal alternative of rustling cattle and delivering these to the government or one of its agents to satisfy contract needs, or after 1879 to the miners at White Oaks. Rustling continued for a time even with the arrival of effective law and order in 1880, this and the appearance of outside capital being the two major breaks with the past.

From about 1879–1880, other parts of New Mexico and the West in general became a field for railroad builders, cattle kings, sheepmen, mining magnates, land barons, and developers of all kinds, fueled by the outside capital that had been almost entirely absent before. The final defeat of the Apache chief Victorio and his followers gave newcomers from the East a sense of security as well, for their persons and the improvements they built or brought with them.

Silver was remonetized in 1878, which made the precious metal worth something again. Mining expanded rapidly and while the Tularosa country had local deposits of coal and gold, it lacked silver. Miners largely bypassed this area apart from the workings they opened at White Oaks (coal and gold) and Capitan (coal). At the same time, imported breeds of beef cattle, particularly Herefords, began to replace the tough, stringy longhorns, mostly through breeding imported bulls to longhorn cows. With the improvement of cattle came stockmen's associations, whereas before it had been every man for himself.

Changes and developments seen elsewhere did not affect the Tularosa country very much, except for the improvements in cattle. Just as important was the failure of internal transportation and communication to improve, beyond the rough roads created by use, until construction of the El Paso and Northeastern Railroad northward to Tularosa and beyond in 1898. Some negative effects were felt as well. As early as 1880, the arrival of the Santa Fe Railway in northern New Mexico allowed the army at Fort Stanton to buy alfalfa for its horses from contractors who shipped it from Kansas to Las Vegas, New Mexico, and then freighted it south to the fort, for less than the cost of corn grown locally by farmers along the Rio Bonito Valley.[49]

New people did arrive, mostly small ranchers and farmers from Texas who homesteaded in the narrow valleys of the Sacramento Mountains for a generation or two.[50] John Meadows was among the vanguard. The Pecos Valley also received more people, who eventually prospered from the development of large-scale irrigation systems and the building of a railroad, first to Eddy (which became Carlsbad in 1899) in 1891 and then to Roswell in 1894.[51] To the north White Oaks, established at the end of 1879, represented the only real mining in this part of New Mexico, apart from the Organ mining area to the west around San Augustin Pass, where the San Andres and Organ mountain ranges meet. Mining meant an influx of outside money as did the appearance of corporate ranching, represented by the Block (El

Capitan Land & Cattle Co.), VV (Kirby and Cree), and Bar W (Carrizozo Cattle Co.) ranches on the north; and the LFD (Littlefield Cattle Co.), Lea Cattle Co., Eddy-Bissell Livestock Co., Diamond A, and others to the east. The Pecos Valley saw the only blossoming of new communities in decades—Roswell (first settled around 1870) and Eddy.

West of the Pecos Valley, ranching by individuals and corporations together with small-scale farming in the tiny valleys carried on until 1898, when the arrival of the El Paso and Northeastern Railroad and the new communities along it finally broke the isolation and heralded a new era.

John P. Meadows was very much at home in the late nineteenth century. It was a world he knew well, from the time he drifted west to New Mexico because there were no more buffalo to hunt. He needed a job and as he said more than once, "I'll work for anyone who'll give me something to eat!" His experiences were all over the map, figuratively as well as literally, and without mentioning the empire-builders (if he ever met any) he told us about people who were much like himself and the world they lived in.

Meadows's stories took a consistently positive view of his associates, apart from a very few understandable exceptions like John Selman. He almost always included his impressions of people and, as with Pat Garrett, these can be quite insightful. Meadows was an uncomplicated man, not one to turn his back on someone who befriended him, as he told Billy the Kid. He was comfortable living where the old ways continued long after they were lost elsewhere, and in telling about individuals and events that would be peripheral in traditional histories. He kept this attitude until the end of his life, when sickness and financial reverses left him literally penniless, his last stories showing simply acceptance and not anger or bitterness. As one newspaper said, he was possessed of a rugged brand of honesty, and endeavored at all times to treat his fellow men as he wished to be treated. His stories offer us a window into his life and times.

Chapter 1

* ⋆ *

Getting Acquainted

Fort Sumner, Pinos Wells, White Oaks

The time ain't long enough to tell all I know about Billy the Kid. I guess I come into Fort Sumner in 1880—in the spring some time, I think about March.[1] I had had a little bad luck on the plains. I had lost my hat down there and consequently was out on the plains nearly three days without a hat. You can imagine what my face looked like after three days in the sun and wind. My partner's name was Tom Norris. I knew him a long time and will say this for him; a better man never lived than Tom Norris.

When we got into Fort Sumner, Tom went to get me a hat, and while he was gone, I went and throwed my bed [roll] on the ground under a tree and lay down and pulled a red handkerchief over my face. I was feeling mighty bad, and I was suffering something terrible with my face. After a while some fellow came along and give me a kick on the foot. This made me take the handkerchief off my face. The newcomer said,

"Say, pardner, looks like you were up against it."

I said, "Yes, that's the way it feels."

He said, "What's the matter with that face of yourn?"

So I told him my troubles and about my hat. He said, "You can't lay here in that hot sun and wind in that fix."

I said, "I say so, too."

He said, "Get up and come on. I'll give you a room and a cot to lay on."

I thanked him and said I thought I'd better stay right where I was at. You see Tom and me had just crossed the plains, and

I had got so plumb full of creeping vermin that I didn't want to go into his room, and I told him so.

But he said, "Oh, I've had a million on me. Come on."

So he picked up my bed and walked over to one of the old 'dobes belonging to the Fort. He walked into one of the rooms and laid my bed on an old iron cot that was there. I went in and laid down on it.

Then this young man—he was in his early twenties, but rather boyish looking—went over to the Maxwell house and told old lady Maxwell about me. She was a good, kind woman, and when she learned the condition I was in, she came over and looked at me. She had the young fellow go get a sponge and wash my face off good. Then she started in to doctor me back to health again. The job took five or six days, but my face got as good as ever.

That was how I came to meet Billy the Kid the first time. Up to then I had never heard tell of him, much less saw him. When I began to think of getting up and moseying around, I asked Tom Norris about the hat he was supposed to get for me.

"'Fore God, John," he said, "I couldn't find no hat here. Looks like they don't wear them out here."

Billy the Kid heard us talking, and says "I'll give him one" and he did, giving me an old Stetson hat he had. The Kid was around the place for several days and each day came to see that I had something to eat and that my face was doctored. I soon got up and was able to get around. In the meantime Billy the Kid was dealing monte for Pete Maxwell's sheep herders and sheep shearers. This was his game and he was a master at the art of dealing monte.

Kid and I began to get pretty well acquainted. I found out from him that the day he found me laying out under the tree, he also had just come into Sumner. We had come in from different directions. I had got there about nine or ten, coming down from Sunnyside six or seven miles to the north, while Kid had come about eleven from Cedar Canyon on the south.

At this time he was on his good behavior and the officers were not molesting him. I got to talking with him pretty freely, and the more I talked to him, the better I liked him.

And to tell the truth, to many when in life he had quite a little personal charm to his friends. I had a few business dealings with Billy and he always treated me fairly. As we go along I will indicate that the man who is generally chronicled as having turned outlaw really had some excellent traits, along with some of his bad ones. I don't know how many [men] he had killed—in fact, I didn't know then he had killed any—and I didn't care. As a matter of fact, I don't care even to this day. I liked him right off the reel, and I do to this day, though it has been fifty years since Pat Garrett captured him by killing [him].

Time went on, and we heard about a big fiesta taking place at Puerto de Luna, a Mexican settlement a few miles to the north of Fort Sumner. Kid says to me one day, "John, I have just come over from White Oaks, the new mining town down in Lincoln County, and I want to go to the fiesta and deal monte to them Puerto de Luna fellows. I been dealing monte at White Oaks, and I made some money. I want to try my luck up at Puerto de Luna."

Then he went on to tell me that he had forty-two head of cattle, yearlings, calves, cows, and two-year-olds, and he put the question to me, "How would it suit you to work for me a little?"

I said, "Kid, I'd work for anybody, if he would give me something to eat."

He laughed and said he'd give me something to eat and a dollar a day besides if I'd help him take those cattle to Los Portales, where as he put it, he wanted to start a ranch.

I said, "All right, I'll go, just so I get something to eat."

My partner, Tom Norris, had got a job driving the mail buckboard from Fort Sumner to Roswell. Pat Boone had been driving on that line, but they changed him from Roswell to Fort Stanton and Tom Norris stepped into his place from Fort Sumner to Roswell.

So I helped Kid take his little bunch of cows over to Los Portales. The first day's drive with the 40 or more head of cattle brought us to "Stinking Springs."[2] We stayed all night there. From there it took two days pretty hard driving to get to Los Portales. I stayed about ten days alone at Portales with that little bunch of cattle.

But things didn't look good to me, leastways so far as starting a ranch was concerned. First of all, he had only forty-two cattle, a pretty small bunch. In the next place, his location looked like a hide-out. It was in one of the depressions common in that country, which you can't see from a distance. In this particular one, there were some springs and a rock corral, close to a small cave-like opening in the side of the depression.

The next day after we got there, Kid went back to Fort Sumner and then on up to Puerto de Luna. I was left with the cattle. A few days later a man named Pankey came along who lived on the Arroyo Plaza Larga between Fort Sumner and old Fort Bascom.[3] He brought a note from the Kid that said, "John, I have sold that entire outfit, brand and all, to Mr. Pankey, in case he likes it. If he does, count them, tally them out, and collect so much (the note gave the prices for cows, calves, steers, and so on)."

I did just as the note said. Pankey liked the cattle, and I tallied them out and collected just what the Kid had put as the price for each kind. I hadn't been working for the Kid long enough to earn enough for a new hat; so I helped Pankey drive them back part of the way. At Stinking Springs, Pankey pulled out towards home across to what used to be called Hubbell Springs. I helped him to get them started on the trail that headed for his ranch. Then I got my pack horse and headed into Fort Sumner, getting there late in the evening.

At Fort Sumner there was no store nor saloon at that time.[4] An old man by the name of Jack Bell was postmaster.[5] He was an old race rider whom old man Maxwell (Pete Maxwell's father), had had with him for many years.

I don't think I ever saw a rougher bunch of men in my life than I found in Fort Sumner the evening I returned. They were all playing poker and drinking heavily. I got pretty uneasy about the $420.00 of the Kid's money I had in my pocket. I went to Bell's to get a cigar box to put the money in and he didn't have any such thing.

Uncle George Fulgum was running a restaurant there, but he was not in sympathy with the rough element.[6] In fact, they had to bring their whiskey into his place from the outside. I asked Uncle George if he had an old cigar box around anywhere, and he dug around on the shelves awhile and finally found one. I put the money in the cigar box together with a slip of paper that told how many cows, calves, etc., I had sold. Then I went to a spot in the bend of the Pecos River where there were a whole lot of stumps. I selected a big one with a bunch of grass growing around it. I slipped my box under the grass, and then to make doubly sure about marking the spot, I got a rock and laid it on top of the stump.

When I went back and told Uncle George about it, he said, "John, you acted wise. Them men is now over in the Kid's room, drinking whiskey and playing poker. There must be eight or ten, and they have been at it here for two or three days now. They are a pretty rough bunch, all right, and no mistake."

When I got up the next morning pretty early, I found that the men were all gone—evaporated, I might say. I didn't know where they had went, but I knew one thing—I was mighty glad they was gone. I guess from their looks I thought it may have been unhealthy for them to be too conspicuous in the daytime. They were a bunch of outlaws. I did not know a single one of them. They evidently had free and welcome access to Billy the Kid's room.

A day or so later, Kid himself come in from Puerto de Luna. I was sitting on a bench in front of the old man's restaurant, when Kid rode in and got off his horse. He asked me about the cattle, and I said, "Yes, I sold them, and have got the money down there in the bend of the river."

"Well," he says in great surprise, "what's it doing there?"

Then I told him about all those men, and he smiled and said, "I guess I can tell you who they were. There was Tom Cooper, Charlie Bowdre, Tom O'Folliard, Billy Wilson," and he named several others whose names I don't recollect. Then he added, "I don't think you was in any danger from them fellows, especially if you had let them know it was my money you was taking care of."

I went out with him to where the cigar box was, set it up on the stump and opened it. I pulled out the paper and said, "Here's how many cattle you had and how much they brought."

He went over the tally list carefully and then said, "You have got one two-year-old steer too many. But I see you've got the money for him, so there's no kick coming." Then when he finished going over the list, he said, "I see how you done it. You run in a long yearling for a two-year-old steer." Then he laughed and said, "That's pretty good, and you made a $10.00 bill by it." Picking up one of the bills, he handed it to me saying, "John you need it. I think you deserve it too if you can make a cow man like Pankey take a long yearling for a two-year-old."

This generous treatment brought a warm spot in my heart for that boy, and it's there yet. When he was rough, he was as rough as men ever get to be, yet he had a good streak in him. Where he got it, the Lord only knows, and He won't tell. But Kid certainly had good feelings. He done some things I can't endorse; for example when he killed Charlie [*sic;* James] Carlyle. He really had no need for doing that.

Kid, I must admit, was too awful rough at times, but everything in the country was rough right about then. It was, to tell the plain truth, very rough. The country was full of all kinds of bad men from cold-blooded deliberate murderers down to sneak thieves, and everybody just had to take care of himself in his own way. The man that was quickest with his gun was the fellow most likely to come out first best. The Kid was always quick with his gun, but sometimes he was quicker than he ought to have been. He done some things that nobody could endorse, and I certainly do not.

But I have gotten far away from my first meeting Kid at Fort Sumner in 1880, about three years after the Kid had come into those parts. A few days after I had reported to Kid about the sale of his cattle, a man named Doc—at least that is what everybody called him, and nothing more—came into Sumner, saying he had lost six head of horses, two of them being especial favorites.

From the way he talked, you could tell that he thought the Kid was mighty likely to know something about the whereabouts of them horses. Doc claimed he had trailed the horses to where they had crossed the Pecos right below Sunnyside. The Kid couldn't tell him anything about the horses, but, as Doc was the partner of Pankey, Kid turned the talk to the cattle Pankey had bought. The Kid said, "I've sold my forty-two head of cattle to Pankey, and I'll just send him the bill of sale by you." Then he made a bill of sale out, and George Fulgum and I witnessed it.

After Doc had gone, Kid said, "I'll bet them horses are up at Pinos Wells.[7] There's a bunch of thieves laying up there that's most likely got them."

I said, "If that's so, let's go get them. That $100.00 reward Doc offers looks good to me."

The Kid sorter [sort of] put his veto on the plan, saying "I don't care about fooling with it. I want to get back to White Oaks. I won some pretty good money when I was down there last time, and I want to go back."

I told him that maybe we could kill two birds with one stone, as Pinos Wells was on the route to White Oaks. The next morning I got two of my horses, riding one and packing the other. The Kid and I took the trail at the river. He was riding a good horse of his own. It was agreed that if I recovered the horses the reward was all mine—all he wanted was to get back over to White Oaks where he could make some money dealing monte. We ran the trail westerly to Seven Lakes;[8] we found a tank of water two or three miles from the big lake and there we camped that night. The next morning we went on in the direction of the big lake. Soon we went over a hill right east of the big lake. When we got in the vicinity, we saw that the big lake had water in it, and when we got there we found that somebody had camped there before us.

Billy the Kid looked over the camping ground and then said, "These ain't no bunch of cattle thieves. These are Indians, and I wouldn't be surprised if it ain't old Victorio's whole outfit. We ought to have came thirty-six hours sooner. Something would have happened then, and there would have been something doing." Some of their camp fires were still smoldering.

We looked around to see what had been left. All we could find was a new rawhide rope and an old pony that was lame and had his back all skinned up. I said, "I guess we don't need to take him. He don't look like he'd do any body any good."

We went on to Pinos Wells, where Kid was to turn off to White Oaks, and I was to go with him, if we had not found the horses. We got there the next evening. The Indians had made a run-in on some Mexican sheep herders and killed several of them.[9] When we got there, Mexicans were burying the last of the herders who had been found at that time and the country seemed full of sheep wandering without a herder.

We stayed all night at Pinos Wells. The Mexicans treated us royally. Billy the Kid spoke the Spanish language quite fluently and always got along fine with the natives. I could speak Mexican fairly well myself, also.

The next morning we took the trail toward Punta de Agua. Before we got there we came across a herder tending a bunch of fat wethers. He hadn't heard of the Indian depredations and of several herders being killed. We stayed all night with him. The Kid told him of the devilment the Indians had been up to in that part of the country. The next morning we turned south toward Gran Quivira. When we got there fortunately we found quite a tank of water, for it had been raining in that country and the water holes were all full. We got there about the middle of the afternoon and stayed until late the next day to let our horses rest up.

There was a big house at Gran Quivira, in rather a bad state of ruin. It had a cross made of cedar poles on top. We got up on the wall and looked at the cross. I suggested that we take the cross down and examine it but the Kid said: "No, John, it has a history and we'll leave some scientific devil do that."[10]

We had never heard of the old mission at Gran Quivira and it excited our curiosity and interest. What at first appeared to be an old trail leading to the valley to the south, on closer examination [proved?] to be an old irrigation ditch. We took our butcher knives and dug into the bank of the old ditch and

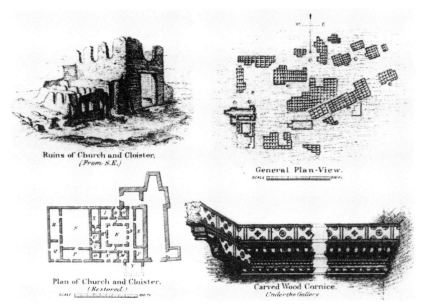

Fig. 4. Gran Quivira, N.Mex. Plan and views by Lieutenant C. C.
Morrison, from Wheeler Survey annual report in Appendix NN of
Annual Report of Chief of Engineers for 1878. Courtesy of the
Museum of New Mexico, neg. no. 190,161.

found it to be caliche, or deposits of lime made by running
water. The ancients must have had sources of water there not
known at present.

What dried up the vegetation, making habitation impossible? I cannot imagine and we could not at that day when Billy
the Kid and I camped at Gran Quivira overnight after stolen
horses. Neither have I ever heard a reasonable theory advanced
that can be substantiated by any known facts. So I will make a
guess which ought to be as good as the next one. I believe that
earthquakes diverted the surface springs and streams under-
ground many ages ago.

When we left there we went to "Red Lake" some 20 or 30
miles southeast of Gran Quivira, hoping to find water.[11] We
found the lake to be dried up. Kid said the next water would
be at the C Dot ranch (now the Bar W) which Tom Catron
owned. We rode all that day without water until we got to

Fig. 5. White Oaks, N.Mex., late nineteenth century. Courtesy of New Mexico State University Library's Archives and Special Collections, Ms0110, Blazer Family Papers, 7.3-28.

Carrizozo Springs.[12] The springs took their name from the reeds that grew in the vicinity—"Carrizozo," Spanish for reeds.

We got there late in the evening, and Kid gave me two silver dollars, saying "You go up there to that ranch and get some grub. Because of what I did in the Lincoln County War, I'm not on good terms with those folks, and I don't want to cause them any embarrassment. I have a chance to get out of all this devilment, and I don't want to get into any more."

He had a letter which he had showed me from the governor, Lew. Wallace, which said that if he came in and stood his trial and was convicted, the governor would pardon him.[13] The governor was doing all he could to bring peace in Lincoln County, and was willing to do anything to get the lawless ones pacified. At least that was the general tenor of the letter.

I went up to the C Dot ranch and the cook gave me some bread and green coffee. (We didn't have the browned and ground coffee then but had to parch the coffee and grind it up in some way. In camp we had to pound the coffee with a stone, piece of iron, or anything handy.) The cook also told me that there was a beef hanging out under the shed and to go out and cut off what I wanted of it. I did so, got the meat, and when I asked him how much it was all worth, including the bread and coffee he told me to take them along and the next time I came that way to stop all night. When I come back and told the Kid, "The old man didn't charge me for this grub. Here's your money," he said, "Put it in your pocket. You may need it. I will set up that much."

We camped there about half a mile from the ranch, and the next day we rode into White Oaks.[14] Who should we find there but the same bunch of rough men I had seen at Fort Sumner. I was introduced to them by Kid. One was Billy Wilson; another was Charlie Bowdre; another was Tom O'Folliard, and still another was Tom Cooper. I don't recall the others. The Kid threw in with them. They had previously been together as a gang, but recently the Kid had not been with them. That was about the time he made a turn for the worse which got him in the mire badly and eventually proved his undoing. I never saw the Kid again until after he had been sentenced to be hanged and came to my place on the Peñasco one night when he was on the dodge.

I didn't care much about being with that crowd [at White Oaks], so I hunted me a job. I went to Uncle John Walters and asked for work about the mine. He said, "I do need a man, but I have no authority to hire any one. LaRue is in charge of the mine, but he is not here. But if you want to go to work, you can do so, and I think you will have no trouble about drawing your pay when LaRue comes in on Saturday."

So I took the chance, and started to work. I worked all week, and when Saturday came LaRue did not appear. He came in Sunday morning, however, but with the report that the mine was in a lawsuit and we would all have to wait for our pay. I may say that I am still waiting.[15]

* * *

Billy and the Lincoln County War

In the many talks Kid and I had, he told me a good deal about what he had been doing. As everybody seems to want to know when and where he killed his first man, I will give what Kid himself told me. I don't remember his saying when, but he did say where. It was at Camp Thomas [*sic;* Camp Grant], Arizona, and the man was an old blacksmith. Kid was there dealing monte—he had run away from his home at Silver City and gone out to Camp Thomas. He had picked up a Mexican partner, and him and the Mexican had gone to a gambling house and dance hall, and made a deal with the proprietor to deal monte. He set up his table, and along comes this old blacksmith, who was broke.

He took a notion that Kid was nothing but a boy and he could manage to get a drink or two off him. So he reached over and tried to take some of Kid's money. Kid slapped his hand away, saying, "Go off and let me alone. Here's two bits. Go get yourself a drink." The old man took the two bits, and people there told me that in September 1880, some of the eyewitnesses told me, and the Kid also told me this.

Presently the old fellow took a notion to have another drink, and tried his old trick. Kid felt this was going too far, and stopped the old man. This made the blacksmith mad, and he slapped Kid down under the table. But when Kid came up from under the table he came up shooting. His bullet went out through the top of the blacksmith's head. This is the way Kid told me himself about the affair, and I heard it the same way from eyewitnesses.

After this Kid and his Mexican partner, Secundo, I think that was the Mexican's name, made a trip down into Old Mexico. They trailed over the old Montezuma trail and down to Chihuahua, where they worked awhile for an old cowman. When they had delivered that herd of cattle, Kid and the Mexican lost their job and came back towards Paso del Norte. When they got near that place, they turned down to Isleta, where this Mexican had relatives.

That cow work in Mexico was the first of that sort of thing Kid had done. But he seemed to like the taste of it, for when he heard that a big outfit at Fort Selden needed hands, he went up there and got in the employ of John Kinney. Kinney had a bunch of stolen cattle, and the Kid didn't like the looks of things. So all he did, as he himself told me, was to play poker a while and win a few dollars. Then he started back for Isleta. As he passed through Las Cruces, he stopped and dealt monte for awhile in the Lapoint Saloon. Lapoint told me this same thing.[1]

Then he went on to Isleta, and got into a difference with his Mexican friend. The Mexican wanted to go on down into the Big Bend country, but the Kid had set his head to go up to Chisum's on the Pecos and see if he couldn't get a job under old John, the cattle king. Kid persuaded the Mexican to come up with him and they come up together through the Guadalupes. One night they camped at Pine Springs, and the next morning the Mexican quit and went back down to Fort Davis.

Kid went on up by himself to Chisum's headquarters at South Spring River, and hung around there awhile. I don't know whether he was regularly employed by Chisum or not, but I think he did join the Chisum outfit in some way. Then he drifted off up the Hondo.

After he left Chisum's he went up on the Ruidoso and, if I remember right, he stopped with Frank and George Coe. Whether this is just right or not, I don't and can't say, but he told me about living with Dick Brewer and Frank and George Coe. He stayed a few weeks with them, and then went over on the Rio Feliz to work for Mr. Tunstall, the rich Englishman who was starting a cattle ranch over there. The Lincoln County War

Fig. 6. William Bonney, "Billy the Kid," photograph prob-
ably taken at Fort Sumner, N.Mex., about 1879.
Copy from G. B. Anderson's *History of New
Mexico: Its Resources and People, vol. 1* (Los
Angeles: Pacific States Publishing Co., 1907).

was brewing, and it seems like it had to come. The country was full of hard men, just as hard as they could be, and there was bound to be trouble, sooner or later.

One day about the middle of February [1878], Billy the Kid and three others who worked for Tunstall went along with him on a trip from the ranch on the Feliz to Lincoln plaza. They went over the old Ham Mills trail that made a short cut through the mountains. A posse of men, some living on the Pecos, some on the Peñasco and at other places in the lower part of the county, overtook Tunstall and his companions. In this posse were Tom Hill and Jessie Evans, two of as bad men as were in the country.

Tunstall started to run, but Hill pulled his gun and said, "Tunstall, don't run. I will protect you." Tunstall reconsidered, according to the way Buck Powell, who was in the posse, told me. Then Hill told Tunstall to come up where he was. Hill sat on his horse and waited for Tunstall to come closer. Then Hill himself killed him. That affair shows the kind of people we had in the country. The killing of Tunstall helped to open up the Lincoln County War. A cold-blooded murder like that will stir up bad feeling anywhere, and that is exactly what happened in Lincoln County.

While I am talking about the Jessie Evans crowd and their doings, I might as well go on and tell what became of Hill after he killed Tunstall. It will help to give an idea of the turbulent ways of the country. The posse that had followed after Tunstall broke up after the killing. The Pecos people turned around and went home. Evans and Hill went on over to the west side of the mountains. An old German named Wagner was driving a large number of sheep from California over into the Concho River section of Texas. It was reported he had a large sum of money at his camp in the mouth of the Alamo Canyon, [with]in three miles of where Alamogordo is now, between the old Alamo Ranch and the mouth of the canyon. So Evans and Hill concluded they would pay the old man a visit. They thought it would be an easy job for the old man was not supposed to know anything about handling a gun. He was trying to get to the Staked Plains of Texas to get range.

When Evans and Hill got to the camp, the old man simply gave up, and they proceeded to hunt for the money he had with him. Hill investigated the wagon. He leaned his gun against the wagon wheel, and then stepped on the wagon brake and on into the bed of the wagon. There he saw a trunk, which he thought might have the old man's money. He stomped on the lid with his boot heel and broke it open. The first thing he seen was a looking glass, and he could not resist picking it up and looking at himself. He called out to Jessie Evans, "Here's a looking glass. I didn't know I was such a fine looking robber, but I'm a daisy."

Then Jessie, he had to have a look, too. "I want to see myself," he said, and went over to the wagon. The Dutchman [*sic*] saw his chance while they were looking at themselves in the glass. He picked up Tom's gun, and killed him with it, literally blowing his spine to pieces. He could have killed Jessie Evans, too, had it not been for the fact that the old man did not know how to reload. When he finally did get a cartridge in place, he took a shot at Jessie, but only managed to wound him in the wrist. And the Dutchman got the horses and saddles and all.

Hill was killed about five or six miles from La Luz. Antonio Baca was justice of the peace then, and he told me all about it himself. Jessie Evans did not deny it, but told old man Frederick about it. He went to Three Rivers near where this [his] friend Felipe Frederick lived in the Nogal Canyon. Frederick heard that Jessie was wounded, and so he went over with his tram and brought him to his home. Billy Mathews was my authority for this.

The government had some kind of complaint against Jessie Evans—I guess it must have been for stealing horses from the Indians; so he was arrested and carried to Fort Stanton. They put shackles on him and let him go around loose. But Jessie managed to cut his shackles off and he with two other prisoners he had got in with, made their escape, stole some horses and pulled for Texas.

They done pretty well until they got to Fort Stockton. They stopped there and tried to rob an old German named Caylor.

They got into his store, took his money, and proceeded to help themselves to clothing and other things a man needs on a trip. But Jessie never made a bigger mistake than when he took in old Caylor. Captain W. D. Roberts was near by with some Texas Rangers and he proceeded to round up Jessie Evans and his companions and send them to the penitentiary. Captain Roberts told me himself about making the arrest.

Now I must get back to my story and tell how the Kid got mixed up with the Lincoln County War. That is kind of a hard question. You will just have to take my opinion and it might be wrong, but I think I am about right. The Kid hadn't thought much about turning his war dogs loose until after his employer Tunstall was killed. That made him start to killing anybody that had taken part in that miserable affair. The Kid told me himself that he had had nothing to do with the troubles in Lincoln County until after Tunstall was killed.

Tunstall had treated him well—had given him some presents I believe, a saddle or a gun, possibly. Kid was like any other boy of seventeen or eighteen, and he worshiped Tunstall for his kindnesses. So when Tunstall was killed, Kid made up his mind to get revenge. I guess he carried out his purpose, for when things didn't go to suit him, he didn't know anything else but his gun. In my opinion, that is what put him into the Lincoln County War.

Billy Morton and Frank Baker [who were other members of the posse that killed Tunstall] were arrested below Roswell by Dick Brewer, Kid, Tom O'Folliard, and several other fellows that I don't remember the names of. The crowd started to Lincoln with the two prisoners. They got about half way between Thirteen Mile Lake and Black Water in a pretty little valley and killed both prisoners. Perhaps I should use a stronger term and say murdered them. Kid told me later, "When we killed Morton and Baker, I had revenge for Tunstall." He thought that they were the ones who had killed Tunstall, and I suppose he continued under that impression up to the time of his own death. That makes, it seems to me, some excuse for the deed, for Kid killed them thinking that they, especially Morton, had killed his friend.

Kid was not the only one who got mixed up in the war. The Coe boys, Dick Brewer, and a good many others all got mixed up in it and went to killing. One side was just about as dangerous as the other, and both sides contained good honest men who believed their course was the right one.

Mr. Brady, the Sheriff, must have been a pretty good man or he would not have been elected sheriff. I don't know much about his getting killed. About six weeks after Tunstall was killed, Billy the Kid and several others of his party waylaid Major Brady in Lincoln and killed him and his deputy [George] Hindman. Kid told me all about that affair. He said, "There was three or four of us shooting at Brady, and I don't know which of us killed him. But I am the one who seems to be blamed for it. Just why I should be picked out I don't know." Kid also said that the killing of Brady raised the bad blood higher and higher between the two parties. It seemed like all the men lost their reason and could not find it again.

McSween was killed in the fight at Lincoln in July 1878 that lasted several days, almost a week. It was more of a siege than an out and out fight. McSween and ten or twelve of his side were surrounded in McSween's home, a large adobe house, by the other side, led by George Peppin, the sheriff. Dolan finally got the soldiers down from Fort Stanton, and they placed themselves in such a position as to make it impossible for the men in McSween's house to do any shooting at the other side without firing into the soldiers.

Colonel Dudley, the commanding officer [at Fort Stanton], had notified McSween that if any shooting at the soldiers occurred, he would turn loose the cannon he had with him and blow the McSween house down. But some of Peppin's men set the house on fire, determined to drive those inside out in much the way that as a boy back in Alabama I used to smoke rabbits out of a hollow tree in which they had taken refuge.

When night came, McSween had reconsidered and was ready to surrender. But Kid and others objected, saying that there was a good chance to slip out under cover of the darkness and get across the Bonito. When they made the dash out of the back door of the house, John [*sic;* Robert] Beckwith shot McSween and the latter fell forward into the yard. In telling me about this, Kid said, "I saw McSween shot and I know who shot him. I was in the smoke of the house behind McSween and they were on the outside. They couldn't see in but I could see out. I took deliberate aim at Beckwith's left eye, and I believe I hit him." I believe he did so myself, for the accounts I heard about the wound in Bob Beckwith's head tallied with such aim as the Kid described.

I think I can explain the real cause of the Lincoln County War. I know that several reasons have been given, but I do not think enough stress has been placed upon the Feliz ranch as the main cause. Tunstall was taking it up for his cattle ranch and Murphy and Dolan wanted it too. It was as valuable a piece of property for stock purposes as there was in New Mexico, and became the bone of contention between these two elements in Lincoln County.

The only way that Murphy and Dolan could get it was to get Tunstall out of the way. So they engineered it and had him killed, but then things opened up right in that section. They found they had to get rid of McSween, Tunstall's business associate and lawyer taking care of Tunstall's estate, and in their efforts to do so they brought the whole section into a most lawless state for several months.

I do not think those who were doing the fighting really understood what it was all about. I once told Kid, "I don't believe either side knew what the fighting was for." He replied, "All I was fighting for was because they killed Tunstall." But I am sure that the Feliz ranch was an important factor. Dolan and his friends finally got the ranch.

A sequel of the Lincoln County War was the killing of John Jones at the old Pearce [*sic;* Pierce] ranch near Carlsbad.[2] Bob Olinger and John Jones had some difference. I don't know just what it was but am under the impression it was a personal affair. They had been fighting together in the Lincoln County War, but afterwards they had had some sort of falling out. When they happened to meet at the Pearce ranch, John Jones offered to shake hands with Bob Olinger. Bob, however, caught John's right hand with his left, jerked his six-shooter and shot John in the back of the head.

The bullet went entirely through John Jones's head and hit M. [Milo] L. Pearce who was lying on a cot in the room. Pearce was struck in the thigh and made a cripple for life. He traveled all over the country in an effort to get his lameness cured—went to New York even, and must have spent a nice little fortune trying to get that bullet removed. Finally he concluded he would not fool with it any more and simply hobble around the rest of his life. Some years afterward, when he was eating dinner, he felt something queer about his leg. He reached down and felt along it. There was something hard just under the skin. He pinched it between his fingers and, ripping his clothes off, he cut into the skin with a butcher knife. In this way he got the bullet out, but the lameness remained. People used to call him "Limpy" Pearce on account of it.[3]

Chapter 3

⋆

Pat Garrett and Billy the Kid

Now I will go on and tell how Pat Garrett came to start to hunting Kid. I knew Pat Garrett for twenty-two years and during practically all of that time we were connected either directly or indirectly. For a good part of the time I was a deputy under him, and I think I know Pat Garrett as well as anybody now living. He was a different sort of man from what some writers make him out to have been. I found Garrett to be a very different man to what they showed here in this moving picture and my picture don't corroborate with that.

Garrett himself told me time and time again that when he was elected sheriff of Lincoln County, his first object was to put an end to Kid's continued defiance of the law without any bloodshed. He said, "I had figured out just how to do it. Before I was elected sheriff, I saw Kid and talked it over with him. We had a game of poker together, and while we were playing, I told him the best thing he could do was to get up and be gone three or four years. Then he could come back and there would be nothing said or done about what had happened in the Lincoln County War. But the Kid could not see the point of my advice, and decided to stay."

At that time Kid was going it alone; he wasn't with Charlie Bowdre and the others that later made up what came to be called his gang. But when they had all gotten together, Pat Garrett still tried his best to get them to leave the country. Garrett arranged a meeting with Charlie Bowdre out on the San Juan Mesa.[1] The agreement was that they were to meet unarmed and talk things over. But Bowdre came with his six-shooter on. Garrett did not like that, and he scolded Bowdre, saying, "Look here, you've betrayed my confidence. You've come armed." But Garrett went ahead anyhow with the meeting. He said to Bowdre, "The best thing all of you boys can do is to leave the country. Why don't you do like Frank and George Coe? Go off to one side and stay awhile; then come back when this thing is over."

Charlie Bowdre promised Garrett that was what they would do. But they did not do it, although Garrett had told them plainly, "If you fellows don't go away, I'm going to arrest you or kill you, or you are going to kill me." They stayed around in the northern part of the county, and finally in the summer of 1880 dropped into the Red Cloud ranch, which was in the vicinity of White Oaks.

Now White Oaks, though a mining town and a pretty wide open place, had a number of people who were determined that the lawlessness that had overrun the other parts of the county should not get a foothold there. They looked askance at Kid and his crowd, although up to that time they had not done anything more than come in and tear around a little.[2]

But while the Kid's crowd was at the Red Cloud ranch, a posse of White Oaks men went out to arrest him on some of the old warrants. Charlie [sic; James] Carlyle went into the house where Kid and his men were. He had gone to school with Billy Wilson, who was in Kid's bunch, and hoped to influence them to give up. While Carlyle was in the house, somebody let a gun go off accidentally on the outside. The Kid's outfit thought a fight was starting right then, and they promptly killed Charlie Carlyle.

This was sort of a last nail in Kid's coffin. It stirred pretty strong sentiment against him. Kid himself regretted it, for he said to me, "We hadn't ought to have done it." But it was done, and after that trouble began to come thick and fast for the Kid.[3]

The Panhandle cattle came into the story next. These cattle bearing the brands of several well known outfits in the Panhandle, these LX, LITS, and LS and another brand or two, I don't remember, but I do remember those, had been stolen and carried over into the vicinity of Tularosa. I happened to be the one to discover their presence there. In February [*sic;* January of 1881; see chapter 6] I had gone to work for Pat Coghlan and he had sent me out to Three Rivers. The first thing I done was to go around over the range and get acquainted with it. I went up on Indian River and found about forty-five head of cattle there with brands that were different from Coghlan's.

About March or April, Pat Coghlan and I had a falling out, and he discharged me and paid me off. The last thing I said to him was "Them LX, LITS, and LS cattle will be bellowing around your bed-post the first thing you know."

All this has nothing to do with Kid, for I don't believe he had anything to do with driving those cattle, although Tom Hill [*sic;* Cooper] and Charlie Bowdre, members of his crowd, had brought them over and sold them to Coghlan. The Kid was over here and I was on the west side of the mountains, but Garrett was trying to arrest them. Charles Bowdre wouldn't listen to Garrett. Maybe Kid did have a hand in it, though I hardly see how he could have, when to my certain knowledge he was right then dealing monte at White Oaks.

After I left Coghlan's employ, I went over across the mountains and bought a ranch on the Peñasco from a man named Haydon, now the Bryan ranch. I got my old partner, Tom Norris to come over and join me. We went to farming together that year. Every once and a while, news filtered down to us how Garrett was chasing the Kid's gang. The Panhandle people had sent some men to New Mexico to get those cattle, and part of Garrett's posse was composed of those Panhandle fellows.

At Fort Sumner, one night, Garrett and his men waylaid the Kid's crowd. Garrett's men were waiting at the corner of an adobe wall, when Kid's band came riding into town. Kid had been in front with Tom O'Folliard, but just before they reached the spot where Garrett and his men were waiting, Kid had a hunch, I guess, for he said, "I want to smoke a cigarette" and dropped back to do so. At any rate it was lucky for him that he did so, for when the posse attacked, Tom O'Folliard got killed.

Kid's crowd broke and run, and made their way back to Stinking Springs. Garrett himself told me how a few days later, his posse surrounded the rock house at Stinking Springs in the night and waited until morning to see if they could capture the rest of the gang. It was in December, near to Christmas, and the ground was covered with snow. Kid and his companions had tied their horses around the house.

When daylight came, Charlie Bowdre put on Kid's hat and went out to see about the horses. As he walked out, Garrett shot him, giving him a death wound. Bowdre staggered up to Garrett, put his hands on his shoulders, and said, "Pat, I wish—I wish—" but fell dead before he could finish his remark. My guess is that he was trying to say to Garrett that he was wishing he had done what Garrett had told him to do out on the San Juan Mesa.

Kid got his horse into the house. Tom Pickett tried to do the same with his horse, but Garrett shot it and broke its neck. The horse fell in the door and blocked it so that Kid could not carry out his intention of getting on his own horse and making a dash after dark.

Garrett thought it was a good time to talk terms of surrender. He said "You fellows have nothing to do but surrender. You better say 'I'll surrender.'" Billy Wilson answered, "All right, I will surrender," and he was the first to come out and give himself up. He was followed by Tom Pickett and the others. Kid was the last one to come, and just before he came out the door Pat called out to him, "Now, Kid, when you come, be sure and come with your hands up."

Kid answered, "All right. I will come with some of them up." When he came out, he would put up first one hand and then the other, and as Garrett himself told me, he would not put up both hands at the same time.

Garrett disarmed them all and took the bunch of prisoners first to Fort Sumner, and then on to Las Vegas. In my opinion he did this because he knew it was not safe to take them to Lincoln. The jail was so poor and there were so many enemies of them there, he could not well keep them at Lincoln. So he pulled for Las Vegas, expecting to go on and place them in the jail at Santa Fe.

When Garrett put his prisoners on the train for Santa Fe, a mob of two or three hundred people surrounded it and tried to take the prisoners and lynch them. Pat picked up his gun and walked out on the platform of the car, and said, "I know what this crowd means. I will kill the first one that puts his foot on the train. Then I will arm my prisoners and fight it out." Kid, in telling me about this incident, said, "I would have given my life if I could have smelled powder burn again there at Las Vegas."

Pat Garrett got his prisoners to Santa Fe and lodged them in the jail. There he stopped, for he had done all his duty. Kid was tried in April at La Mesilla, the county seat of Doña Ana County, and sentenced to be hanged at Lincoln in a month for the killing of Sheriff Brady. He had to be taken back to Lincoln County and that put him into Pat's hands again.

Billy Mathews, Bob Olinger, Jim Bell, and Dave Woods were the guards that took Kid over to Lincoln. But when they got there, they did not put the Kid in the jail. They put him in the sheriff's office in the upstairs of the courthouse with Bell and Olinger to guard him. When Kid got to Lincoln, he had on little short shackles in which he could hardly take a step. Garrett, who was still disposed to treat Kid kindly, said, "It is not necessary for that boy to have them short shackles on. You can take care of him with longer ones just as well, and they will make it much more comfortable for him."

Bell was kind and considerate of Kid, but, as Kid himself told me, Olinger was mean to him. In talking about it to me, Kid said "He used to work me up until I could hardly contain myself. But Bell was a nice little fellow, who always treated me well. When I made up my mind how I was going to try to get away, I decided I would not harm Bell in any way if I could help it."

The day before Kid made his escape, Olinger loaded his shot-gun with twelve buckshot, remarking as he did so, "The little, hazel-eyed ——————— will be pretty apt to stop, won't he, Kid, when he gets these?"

Kid said, "I expect he will; but be careful, Bob, or you might shoot yourself accidentally."

Bob went over to the hotel across the street to get his dinner. The Kid waited until Bob was settled at his dinner, and then he made an excuse to be taken by Bell down to the privy which was in the yard of the jail. Bell, of course, went along, but as they came back, he lagged some distance behind.

When Kid found he had turned the short turn at the bottom of the stairs and was not closely followed by Bell, he said to himself, "Here's my opportunity. I will either get killed or escape." The shackles he was wearing were right for his effort. They enabled him to make two or three quick jumps and reach the top of the stairs. As Kid was doing this, he slipped his handcuffs off, something he always could do easily, since he had large wrists and small hands.

When Bell got to the head of the stairs, Kid met him, and slapped at the side of his head with the handcuffs. The blow stunned him, and the two went to the floor in a scuffle over Bell's gun. What Kid wanted to do was to make both Bell and Olinger prisoners, and handcuff them together while he was making his escape. The first step towards this end was to get hold of Bell's gun.

Kid got Bell's pistol and tried to hold Bell. But Bell got loose, and started back down the stairs. Then Kid shot him. Kid told me exactly how it was done. He said he was lying on the floor on his stomach, and shot Bell as he ran down the stairs. Kid said of this killing, "I did not want to kill Bell, but I had to do so in order to save my own life. It was a case of have to, not of wanting to."

After killing Bell, Kid went into the sheriff's office and picked up the same shot-gun Olinger had loaded the day before. Then Kid went into the northeast corner room of the building, and took his station at a window from which he could see Olinger when the latter came back from dinner. Olinger had heard the shot that killed Bell and was hurrying back to the jail to see what it was all about.

Kid waited for Bob to open the gate which was right under the window of the room where Kid was. Kid heard the gate slam as Olinger passed through it, and he heard at the same time Alex Nunnelly shout to Olinger, "Bob, Kid has killed Bell."[4] What happened next I will give just as Kid told it to me. He said, "I stuck the gun through the window and said,

'Look up, old boy, and see what you get.' Bob looked up, and I let him have both barrels right in his face and breast."

After he killed Olinger, Kid come back to the hall on the second floor and walked to the window at the south end of it. He called to a German named Gauss, whom he saw in the yard back of the jail, "Gauss, pitch me up that old pick-axe lying out there, and let me get this chain between my feet broke in two with it."

Gauss pitched it up to him, saying, "Look out, Billy, here she comes." Kid caught it and went to work on the chain to his leg shackles. That is how Kid told it to me. When he had got the chain broke in two, he pulled up the loose ends of the chain and fastened them to his belt so that they would be out of the way in walking.

Then he went to the north end of the hall, in front of which was a little porch. He sat on the bannisters [*sic*], whistled and sang and made a short speech to the people who had gathered around but were too much afraid to get very close or to make any effort to impede the Kid's escape. He said, "I am going to give the good people of Lincoln a chance to think a little. I'm not going to hang on the day they have been expecting I would." Then he reached down inside his boot and pulled out a little paper enclosing some white stuff. He threw the contents of the paper on the ground, saying "I don't think I'll need that now." Dr. Tomlinson, who examined some of it afterwards, said it was crystallized strychnine. So I guess the Kid didn't intend to hang noway.

The Kid went back into the building and descended by the inside stairs to the back yard. He said to Nunnelly, "Go saddle Billy Burke's horse for me and bring him here. I need him."

Nunnelly said, "I want to do that, Kid, bad enough for you, but I've got to be tried myself in a few days for killing two Mexicans on Tulerosa [*sic*; Tularosa] Creek. Don't you reckon my helping you will make it go harder with me?"

Kid said to him, "You can tell them I made you do it, for that is just what I am going to do."

Then Nunnelly said, "Well, I guess I might just as well go and saddle him."

When Kid tried to mount, the horse pitched him off, and kept on bucking around the yard. Kid called to the old Dutchman, Gauss, "Gauss, go get that horse, and bring him back here. I can ride him."

Gauss did so, and when Kid tried to mount the second time, he handed Gauss his gun to hold. The horse kept up the bucking, but the Kid rode him all the same. When he had the horse under control, he rode up to Gauss, and said, "Now, Gauss, old boy, give me my gun."

"Here it is, Billy," he said.

Kid took the gun and rode off, saying, "Good-bye, Gauss, I may never see you again."

Gauss waved his hat at him, and shouted, "Good-bye, Billy, you ——————."

Kid rode over to [Scripio] Salazar's ranch or some other place on the north side of Capitan Mountain. He staked the horse to an amole [yucca] stalk, and that night the horse jerked the stalk up and went back to Lincoln with the saddle on. There was still a portion of the dagger bush on the end of the rope. It is quite certain in my mind that the horse got away before the Kid was through with him. Old Man Salazar let the Kid have a little sorrel horse and a good one, and also a saddle. He hung around for a day or so under cover in the hills and one night after dark he showed up at Tom Norris' and my ranch, on the Peñasco about four miles below where Elk now stands. Kid told me all this three or four days later.[5]

I remember how he made his appearance at the place. Tom Norris and I was in the cabin cooking some supper. Kid come up to the corner of the house and seeing that there was nobody there but us two, whom he could trust, he stepped to the door and said, "Well, I've got you, haven't I?"

I said, "Well you have. So what are you going to do with us?"

He said, "I am going to eat supper with you."

I said, "That's all right, if you can stand our beans."

He stayed in the house and ate supper with us. But he wouldn't stay there long so we all three went out onto a little hillside to talk matters over. I told Billy we would get in bad with the law if we harbored him and he told me that he didn't expect us to hide him out. While he was with us, he told me everything I have given in this account,—the arrest at Stinking Springs, the excitement with the mob at Las Vegas, and all the other matters I have told about.

At that time I was not well acquainted with Pat Garrett. I had met him and that was all; but I knew he was hunting for Kid. So I asked some questions. I said, "Tell me, Billy, didn't you come here to kill Billy Mathews? He was the strong witness against you in the trial, I understand."

"Yes," said Kid, "he was. But it would be a pity to kill him. I'll give you my word that if I met him out on the hills, I wouldn't kill him."

Then I asked the same question about Pat Garrett. Kid's answer was equally generous, "If I was laying out there in the arroyo, and Pat Garrett rode by and didn't see me, he would be the last man I would kill. I wouldn't hurt a hair of his head. To be sure, he worked pretty rough to capture us, but he treated me good after he got me. Ever since, I have a good feeling for Pat Garrett."

I had to ask Kid one more question about his feelings toward another of his enemies. "What kind of feeling," I asked, "do you have for Bob Olinger?"

His reply was brief but very emphatic. "I expressed that the other day," he said, and then proceeded to tell me how he had killed Bob Olinger, which was the first I had heard of it.

We talked until eleven o'clock that night. I said, "Kid, when I was sick and down and out at Fort Sumner, you befriended me. There is two things I have never done. I have never kissed the hand that slapped me and I have never went back on a friend. And I'm not going to begin either of them now. I am going to befriend you to the end."

"Tom and me have got fourteen head of old Indian ponies. Some of them ain't very much, but you can go out and look them over, and if one of them seems likely to do you any good, take it. In fact you are welcome to all of them. But whatever you do, don't go back to Fort Sumner. Garrett will get you sure as you do, or else you will have to kill him."

He said, "I haven't any money. What could I do if I went to Mexico or some other place with no money? I'll have to go back and get a little before I can leave."

I repeated what I had said, "Sure as you do, Garrett will get you, or you will have to kill him."

He said, "Don't you worry. I've got too many friends up there. Anyhow I don't believe he will try to get me. I can stay there awhile and get enough to go to Mexico on."

I said, "You better go while the going is good. If you go back up there, you will either get killed or kill Garrett."

I couldn't make him change his mind, and Kid went back to Sumner with the consequences I shall now tell. Garrett got a tip that Kid was there. He was tipped off by one of the Kid's friends. Then Garrett got John W. Poe and Kip McKinney, and they went up to see if the report was true. Garrett thought he could get Kid without killing, and both Poe and McKinney afterwards told me the same thing. They all thought they could slip up on him and capture him without having to kill him.

They went to the Maxwell house about midnight. This house had formerly been a part of the officers' quarters at the old fort, and was a building perhaps two hundred feet long, cut up by partitions into several rooms. Pete Maxwell was sleeping in the east room. Garrett went into Maxwell's room to ask about Kid.

In the meantime Kid had come in from one of the sheep camps where he had been hiding, and had gone into a room at the west end of the building. There stayed in it an old Navajo woman who had been with the Maxwells a long time, and she was always very friendly toward the Kid.

Kid said to her, "I'm hungry. Haven't you got anything to eat?"

She said, "There's some coffee on the table, but it isn't hot, and there's some tortillas. But if you want more, there is a sheep hanging on the porch. Go get yourself some of that and cook it."

Kid went out to get a piece of meat, and as he was going, he seen some men sitting on the porch in the shadow. He stepped off across the ditch, and went around them, saying

Fig. 7. Old Fort Sumner, N.Mex., in 1883. Pete Maxwell's house, where the Kid was killed, is in left-center background. Courtesy of the Museum of New Mexico, neg. no. 1818.

"Quién es?" (Who are you?). Kip McKinney answered back in Mexican, "It is nobody that wants anything with you. Go tend to your own business."

Kid come on over to Pete Maxwell's room to ask him what he knew about those men on the porch. Maxwell was lying on the bed and Pat Garrett was sitting on the side of the bed talking to him. Kid was in his sock feet; he had taken off his boots when he started to get the meat. He also had in his hand the butcher knife with which he was going to cut the meat.

As soon as he got into the room, Kid said to Pete Maxwell, noticing some one sitting on the bed, "Pete, quién es?"

Pete said in a whisper to Garrett, "I believe that's him."

Garrett jerked his gun, and about the same instant, the Kid drew his and threw it on Garrett just about six inches from him. Then Garrett leaned over to the side a little and shot, his bullet hitting the Kid right in the heart. Kid fell on his back in the moonshine that was on the floor of the room.

I was not in Fort Sumner when this happened, but the next day I come in after a couple of horses of mine that Pete

Maxwell had had for about a year. As I rode into the place I seen right smart excitement, and when I got to Pete's house I asked Pete what it was all about. He said, "We have just buried the Kid. Pat Garrett killed him the other night." He then went on to tell me the circumstances, which were as I have told them. I also had practically the same account from Pat Garrett and John W. Poe. As all of them tally in important particulars, I think it must be the correct account of how Kid was killed.

Pat Garrett was inclined to be kind to Kid to the last. He gave Pete Maxwell the money to buy a suit of clothes and give the Kid a decent burial in other respects.

People nowadays are fond of discussing the comparative merits of these two, Billy the Kid and Pat Garrett. In my mind it is difficult to compare them. Garrett was raised in Louisiana in civilization. Kid was raised in Silver City in the dance hall and the gambling room and the saloon. Kid did not have the favoring circumstances that Garrett had, but there was something about Kid that makes me feel he was pretty well-bred. He must have had good stuff in him, for he was always an expert at whatever he tried to do. He was superlatively good both at shooting monte and six-shooting.

Among some other good traits the Kid had he was quite generous with his friends. Also, others will bear me out in saying that the Kid would not stand to hear any derogatory remarks about any decent woman. Only a few weeks ago Mr. George Coe, who was with Billy's outfit for a year, made the same statement. He [Kid] showed the same humane feelings that we all have. The way he befriended me at the beginning of our acquaintance has always made a warm spot in my heart for that fellow; desperado, outlaw, cattle thief, gambler though he may have been. In my view he was a creature of circumstances. I often wonder how many of those who are now inclined to throw stones at him would have turned out better if they had been brought up under the same conditions?

Of all those in the scrap, the Kid was the one who got the rap. Neither could I exactly ever find out why Billy was the one who needed killing and none of his gang (at the time of the killing of the sheriff, Brady)—George and Frank Coe, Billy Mathews [*sic*; probably Billy Wilson], and a number of others. In a friendly banter I have often told George Coe that he needed killing at one time just as bad as did Billy the Kid. George never seemed to make out a case as to why not—at that time, if Billy did. And speaking further of my old friend, George Coe, it may be said in justice to Mr. Coe [that] he was with the Billy the Kid gang for one year at the time when they believed their cause to be just. Mr. Coe knew Billy most intimately as an associate. And when Billy and some of his men turned to thievery and outlawry, the Coe boys refused to go with them.

I am well aware of the fact that my version of some of the Billy the Kid lore is not in accordance with that of the story writers' and you can do as you please about accepting any of it. I have what I consider good reasons for any of my statements relative to Billy the Kid—I knew him and since that time have talked with a hundred or more people who knew him. Of course, as I have stated, a great deal of my information about Billy was from the mouth of Billy himself.

I knew Garrett for twenty-two years, and I can say with honest conviction that I never met in my life a man who was any more truthful, any more honorable, or any better citizen than he. I was deputy sheriff under him for six years, and stayed at Las Cruces, where he and his family were living. We would differ once in a while over something, but we could always settle it without any sharp words. Garrett was a good man and had a good heart in him. People ought not to blame him for killing the Kid. Garrett did it for self-preservation, and it was one of those things a peace officer sometimes has to do, when he would much rather not.[6]

* ★ *

Seven Rivers and Fort Sumner to Silver City in 1880

In 1880 I hired [out] to Pierce & Paxton at Seven Rivers, to help gather their cattle and drive them to Fort Bascom on the Canadian River. There the cattle were to be turned over to a Nebraska outfit. On the trip up with the cattle, above Bosque Grande, Buck Powell, foreman in charge of the outfit, rode up to me when we were nearing Fort Sumner. He said he had heard a rumor that Billy the Kid and his gang were hanging around Fort Sumner, waiting to seize the cattle we were driving.

I had seen Billy only a few weeks before and I told him that I did not believe that the Kid was planning to do any such thing. I told him I would ride into Fort Sumner and see what I could. I told Buck Powell I thought we could hold our ground against a pretty good sized bunch of outlaws. We got the outfit into the big valley east of Fort Sumner and got onto ground that would favor us if it became necessary.

Mr. Pierce, one of the owners, was with us, but he was crippled on account of a shot he got in the hip from Bob Olinger's gun, as he was after another man [John Jones; see chapter 2]. Olinger, you may recall, was the officer Billy the Kid killed a few months later. I told Mr. Pierce I would go into Fort Sumner and see if I could find out where that bunch of bad men were. There were some pretty tough hombres around Fort Sumner at that time and make no mistake as to that. The most of them came to a bad end in due time, too.

I rode into Fort Sumner. There wasn't much there but a little restaurant run by Uncle George Fulgum. I went in to see him. He knew that Billy the Kid and I had more or less acquaintance, for he had seen us together. I asked him if he knew where the Kid and his partners were, and he replied: "No, damn them, I don't, and I don't want to know." He remarked that the Kid had a good chance to get out of his devilment and had not done it. Now he has gone and thrown in with a bunch of thieves and he can take his medicine.

I went back to the outfit and told Mr. Pierce and Powell what Mr. Fulgum had told me. They talked it over and concluded we would not have any trouble at Ft. Sumner, but might have some at Hubbell Springs, about 25 miles northeast of Ft. Sumner, on the Fort Bascom road. But their fears were groundless. That drove of cattle went through all right to its destination at Fort Bascom. The Nebraska men were there to receive them.

After we turned the cattle over, we went back to Seven Rivers. When I had been in Fort Sumner some time before the cattle drive I had four head of horses that I had left with Pete Maxwell. Of these I took the best of the four with me back to Seven Rivers. At the time Tom Norris, who came with me from Texas, was driving a mail hack [buckboard] between Fort Sumner and Fort Stanton.

A man by the name of [Henry L.] Van Wack [Wyck] had a cow camp near Seven Rivers, about a mile and a half below the place, at a big spring. Tom Johnson, one of Van Wyck's men, had made the drive with us to Fort Bascom. While on the trip, he and I had agreed on a trip to Arizona. I was staying at the Van Wyck camp until we could get started.[1]

We left Seven Rivers the 17th of March [sic; August], 1880, going by way of Peñasco and the Mescalero Indian Agency. At that time there were no houses except some small log houses at the Agency. The Indians had little use for houses then. There was neither [not] a store, and only a government commissary. A bunch of the Indians, who had been off the reservation without leave, had been brought back by the soldiers and were being held under guard on a hillside. The government rationed the Indians liberally, providing them with sugar, flour, beans, etc., in order to keep them pacified and on the reservation.

We came on down to Tularosa and at that time the village of Tularosa was quite a little less than twenty years old. There we got some ripe peaches, the first we had had for three years. We loaded a pack horse with peaches and started on our journey towards Las Cruces. At that time there was a daily mail hack from Las Cruces to Tularosa. We traveled as far as the south point of the White Sands and stayed with old man Maxwell. Maxwell had a government agency and supply depot there and bought his feed and supplies out of Tularosa.

A few days before we stopped with him, he had gone to Tularosa after supplies one day and when he returned he found his two young sons, one 16 and the other 18 years of age, murdered. Some accused the Indians of committing the murder, but many others believed the Indians had not a thing to do with the crime.[2] The old man was so heart-broken that he had concluded to sell out and go back to Colorado. He was a widower and later sold out to Pat Coghlan, who was engaged in businesses of several kinds quite extensively at that time.

The next morning we went on our way to 'Cruces. When we got to the forks of the road where one branch went to Las Cruces and the other to the San Nicholas ranch, we took the 'Cruces road. I was riding up out of the road by the side of the trail and discovered a big splotch of blood on the ground beside the road and also saw where blood had been spattered on the bushes. We looked around and found a trail over which some object had been dragged, leaving blood scattered along [it]. We followed it and in about a half mile came to two dead Mexicans, a man and a woman. They had been killed by the Indians. The Indians had tied ropes to their feet and dragged them to an old lake bed, but had not scalped them.

Later from Las Cruces we found that the man and woman were from Ysleta, Texas, and were traveling with a burro toward Tularosa, where they were going to work for the government. They had been killed by old Victorio's band of renegade Apaches, who were then on the rampage.[3]

We met the stage driver and Johnson, who could talk Spanish, told the Mexican driver what we had just found. That night we camped near the famous Chalk Hills some miles below the point of the sands. Next day we made it to the Shedd ranch, now known as the Cox ranch, where we stayed all night. The next day we made it to where Organ City now stands, on the west side of the Organ Mountains. There was no town there then. We stayed at a spring now known as Cottonwood Spring. The next trek was to Old Fort Selden, 16 miles north of Las Cruces. We stayed most of the next day and greatly enjoyed a swim in the Rio Grande River.

While in the water, Tom Norris found a hot spring, the water coming up out of the bed of the river being quite hot. This was near what is now known as Radium Springs. We speculated considerably over the hot springs and were quite mystified about them.

The next day we went as far as Mason's ranch, about 20 miles west of Fort Selden. There was a government road over which we traveled. In the Mason Hills west of the Mason ranch we passed the spot where old Vic's [Victorio's] band had killed a party of 17 Mexicans and had taken their work steers, a year or so before. These people had not been buried in the ground for some reason but had been laid out and rock piled over them, forming a large mound.[4]

There was an old German peddler right behind these Mexicans. He had a horse team and load of goods which he had purchased of Numa Reymond, the well-known merchant of Las Cruces. He disappeared, horses and all, and at that time no one had ever known what became of the German. He left his wagon, but I don't know whether he got away on a horse or whether the Indians killed him. About twenty years later, when I was a deputy sheriff under Pat Garrett, I found some of the stock of goods belonging to this old peddler in a way that makes a good story.

Old man Carr, who lived seven or eight miles below where this massacre occurred, had come and asked Pat Garrett and me to help him follow some stolen horses. The day after we got to his ranch, we rode a circle around to see if we could pick up the trail of the horses. Going north on the east side of a bluff, I saw something that looked like red chicken feathers, and I stopped and got down and examined it. It proved to be a piece of calico with a little red dot on it. I trailed it back up the rim rock about two hundred yards, and found a place where I could descend onto a bench-like rock formation. This I followed back until I came to a cave back under the rim rock, and there I found several kinds of cloth, calico and other stuff, and also a lot of trimmings, laces, and so on.

One of the bolts had a cost mark label on it, which I took off and carried back to Carr's ranch with me that night. When I got through finding the thieves that had taken his horses—it took three weeks—I came back by way of Carr's ranch and gathered up the price tags I had taken from those goods. When I got to Las Cruces, I showed them to Numa Reymond, who kept a store there, and he exclaimed, "My God, that's my old cost mark that I had in 1880. Those goods were goods I let the old German peddler have to peddle out." But this did not solve the mystery of what happened to the peddler. So far as I have ever heard, his fate is yet unknown. It is surmised that he may have seen the Indians in time to cut a horse loose from the wagon and escape. Or, he may have been murdered as were the Mexicans.

But I must get back to the trip to California [Arizona]. We were two days getting to Fort Cummings, which is south of Cook's Peak and some 18 or 20 miles northeast of what is now Deming. When we got within six or eight miles of the fort, we passed an old Mexican named Montoya, who was cutting hay with a large hoe.[5] We stopped and asked him if he wasn't afraid to be out there on the plains all by himself, when the Indians were so bad? "No," he said, "me and Victorio are good friends. I knew him at San Carlos."

We left him and drove on until we had come within a mile or so of the fort. We had just reached the top of a hill from which we could look over the surrounding country, when we noticed great clouds of dust rising off the ground. Tom Johnson said that it was not just dust—it must be Indians or something. So we stopped and watched developments. Presently they got in sight, and it was Indians sure enough. We watched them until they came up to the poor old Mexican [and] killed him in

Fig. 8. Fort Cummings, N.Mex., c. 1882; primarily a tent camp at this time. Courtesy of the Museum of New Mexico, neg. no. 1678.

cold blood. The band then went south into the south end of the Cook Mountains, and then up into the mountains to one of their retreats.[6]

At that time there were Negro soldiers at the fort, Col. [George P.] Buell commanding them. The commander insisted that we stop and he fed us and our horses over night. In the morning the commander sent a detachment of soldiers to engage old Victorio, but he was too wily for them and they returned to the fort.

Col. Buell invited us to remain until all danger from the Indians was past, but we started on. We came through Cook's Canyon to the Mimbres. When we got to within about half a mile of the Mimbres we could see a large band of Indians up on the mountains to the north of us. They would probably liked to have sacked us but were probably a little afraid of the soldiers. We ran until we got to an old adobe wall where somebody had started to build a house but had never got a roof on it. We went into that—horses and all. We had plenty of good arms and ammunition and were prepared to put up a fairly hard scrap if the Indians came. However, they never made their appearance.

The Indians crossed the Mimbres River five miles distant from where we were and went on to Apache Tejo. At that place there was an ore stamping mill and a colony of miners. The men got out their guns and held the Indians off. We got there the next day in time to help bury the dead. Two Mexicans were killed. This particular band of Indians went from there into Old Mexico, and the most of them were slaughtered later by Mexican soldiers. Apache Tejo was the place where "Apache Bill," a somewhat noted scout and Indian interpreter, was captured by the Indians in 1852. His parents and sister were killed. Apache Bill married a Mexican girl in Tularosa and reared a family. Bill died in the soldiers' home at Sawtelle, Calif., in 1924. At the time of his capture the Indians were going to kill the child, but an old squaw begged so for his life that they gave the child to her. He was recaptured from the Indians in 1862 and was very well versed in Indian lore and the language.[7]

After we passed Apache Tejo we heard of Indian depredations around Silver City. At that time Silver City was getting up a company of vigilantes to drive the Indians out of the section. Judge W. A. Hawkins, now of La Luz, then a young attorney of Silver City, was a member of the company of vigilantes.[8]

Chapter 5

* **

Southern Arizona and Return to New Mexico, 1880

After we left Silver City we saw no more Indians for some time. We came to a little store on the north side of the Gila River called Richmond, now on the south side of the river and known as Duncan.[1] We went on down to where Solomonville, Arizona, is now—it used to be called Pueblo Viejo. It was right on the mouth of the San Simon Canyon and the Everard flour mills were then in existence. There Tom Norris and Tom Johnson and me separated, and I turned back south to the Chiricahua Mountains. There I hired [out] to Ike Clanton to herd cattle, but I did not continue in the job long. I worked about a week or ten days for him, and found out that the cattle had been stolen from Old Mexico.

In the fall (of '80) the Indians had made a raid on the Gila section, but it was not Victorio's band. I tried to get a job with the government but failed. I concluded I would follow the soldiers and Indians for what loose stock I could pick up. The Indians when hard pressed often abandoned a portion of their stock. The soldiers never bothered to pick stock up.

At Willcox the soldiers started south down the Sulphur Springs Valley. Right where Geronimo was captured several years later the Indians, who were followed, went up a canyon. The soldiers did not follow them into the canyon the day they got there. The next morning I ventured up and picked up 14 Indian horses, one government and two big work horses. The Indians being hard pressed had got out and left the stock behind. I found those horses on Canes Creek, and thought I was in great luck. I had all I wanted and went back to Willcox with the stock. There I went into a store and reported what I had. A freighter there from Tombstone remembered the work horses and who they were stolen from; they belonged to a freighter at Tombstone. I later turned the work horses over to the owner and as he was a poor man and had considerable hard luck I accepted no reward. The government horse I got a reward of $100 for.

The Indian ponies and my own horses I took back with me to the spring in what was known as Granite Mt., now known as Tres Hermanas. While at the springs I struck up with Capt. Jack Doyle, whom I had known back in Texas. He was doing some assessment work on mines near there. Then I went to killing deer, elk, and antelope—any kind of game I could kill, and packed it on some of the horses in to the end of the Southern Pacific, which was then at Willcox, Arizona.

Some time in September I made a trip to Camp Thomas [*sic*; again, probably Camp Grant]. While I was there, they had a big government sale of horses and one of the animals put up was a big, fine, red roan which had been condemned for pitching. Tom [Johnson?] and me bought that horse off the line. We carried him into a corral, put a saddle on him, and undertook to ride him. I tried first but he pitched me off. Hardly had I hit the ground, when Tom ran and jumped on him, but he too got pitched off. I caught the horse, but before mounting again, I pulled the cinch up as tight as I could. Then I got on and rode him. I broke him of pitching.

At this time Tom had gone to driving a stage from Camp Thomas to Willcox, but on one of his trips he was taken sick when he got there. He had a case of light typhoid fever, but it lost him the position with the stage company. When he was able to go back to work, Joe Colynon, who ran the Sutton outfit at the time, put Tom on his cow ranch up in the Green Mountains, and that was the last time I saw Tom until he came back to Lincoln County, N.M., a good many years afterwards.

Just at this time I met two old Texas cowpunching friends of mine, named Bill and George Graham. It was a curious fact that George and me were both born on the same day, the 26th of May, 1854. When we met in Arizona, I told him what a great

Fig. 9. Pat Coghlan (seated) and a Lieutenant
Norton, n.d. Courtesy of New Mexico
State University Library's Archives and
Special Collections, Herman Weisner
Papers, C/1/5a.

country Lincoln County, New Mexico was, and we concluded
we would go back. During this time the soldiers had run
Victorio back into Mexico, and a little later he was killed down
there by Mexican troops. This relieved us of having any trouble with the Indians on our way back.

In a few days, Bill and George Graham came into my camp
and had 7 or 8 horses of their own. I had about the same
number. We had a little money between us, and were able to

make a trade for a California wagon—what was called a three-inch wagon. We also traded some of our horses for some old "stove-up" stage horses, the reason being that not all of the horses we had were suitable for driving, not being broken to the harness. We hitched four of the stage horses to the wagon and prepared to start back to New Mexico. But they were the balkiest things I ever saw; not one of them would tighten a trace. When we concluded they would not pull with harness, I cut up a stake rope into pieces about four feet long and tied one end to the horses' tails and the other to the trace. We made them pull almost all the way back to New Mexico that way.

The night we camped at Cook's Peak on the way back happened to be the day Victorio was killed. The news had come by the telegraph to Rincon on the Santa Fe, and it had been relayed to the town of Colorow [*sic*; Colorado?], which was not far from the peak. We happened to go down to it that night, and heard the news from a man, Pacopa, who had a store at Colorow.[2]

The Graham boys and me came to New Mexico with the intention of getting work from the John Chisum outfit at Seven Rivers, but as there seemed to be nothing doing in this part of the country, they concluded they would go back to Arizona. We stayed at Seven Rivers for six weeks or two months. Then we divided up our horses and other stuff. They gave me the wagon and the celebrated stage horse team, and another horse, a saddle horse, to go with them. This was the first of 1881. After the Graham brothers went back to Arizona I did not hear from them for a number of years. The next [time] I did run on to them was at Hope, N.M., a few years later where they were in the stock business. Bill Graham died at Hope and is buried there. George went back to Arizona again and went into the cow business there, along about 1905. The last I heard of him he owned a ranch up northeast of Phoenix

After they left I got a little job here and there wherever I could. Before Christmas I had sold the four horse team and the wagon for $180, and two head of saddle horses. That's really what I got for them. There was nothing doing on the Pecos River just then, and I wrote to Tom Norris back at Camp

Thomas to gather up what he had and come back to the Peñasco, where we might buy a small ranch. He wrote back that he could not come until the next July—it was then somewhere near Christmas. So I concluded I would go back to where he was. When I got as far as Tularosa, Pat Coghlan hired me to work on his Three Rivers Ranch with his cattle. I sold my pack horse, but kept the saddle horse, and went to Three Rivers to work for old Pat.[3]

I Go to Work for Pat Coghlan

I commenced working for Coghlan about the first of January in '81. He had sent me out to Three Rivers. When I got there the first thing I did was to ride over the range in order to learn it as well as I could and see the general condition of things. I found between forty and fifty head of cattle that were clearly stolen. They were branded LIT mostly, though some were LFB and LX (connected). I knew that these cattle belonged to outfits in the Panhandle, and I told Mr. Nesmith, the foreman, what I had seen, saying, "I found something today that does not look good to me."

He says, "What?"

I says, "A bunch of stolen cattle on Indian River."

He says, "What brand?"

I told him what the brands were, and he said those were the cattle Pat Coghlan had bought from Tom Cooper and Charlie Bowdre.

I thought it my duty to old Pat to call his attention to the fact [that the cattle were clearly stolen] and advise him not to fool with them. He said it would be all right to go ahead and issue those cattle on his contract over at Fort Stanton, and promised that he would stand the brunt. I told him that I had had two men standing the brunt for me back in Texas, but I had found that I had to do most of the riding. He promised to make the matter right, and we dropped the discussion of it for a time. I felt sure that these were cattle he had bought from Tom Cooper and Charlie Bowdre the year before.

About the 1st of February, he sent word to me to come down into town from the ranch. I came in the next day, saw Pat, and started back the next day to the ranch. On the return trip I met Charlie Siringo out at Temporal.[1] He had stayed at the ranch the night that I spent in town. We had met each other in the Panhandle a year or so previous, and recognized each other as old acquaintances. We got down from our horses and sat on the ground and had a good confab. He had come into that section as a detective for the cattlemen's association in the Panhandle. Charlie got confidential and told me that he was looking for stolen cattle with just the brands I had noted on Coghlan's cattle.

I then told Charlie all about the brands and everything, and he asked me what sort of a man Coghlan was? I answered that I was not sure whether I had the man down right or not, but my private opinion publicly expressed would be that he was a dishonest and unfaithful man. Siringo ended the talk by saying, "I will go to Tularosa tonight. Don't let anyone know we are acquainted, and I will see you again later on." He did as he said, went to Tularosa, saw Coghlan, and asked about the cattle. Coghlan pretended that he knew nothing of any such cattle, and Charlie came back to the ranch where I was that night.

The next day we said nothing to each other one way or another about the cattle, but Charlie quietly got on his mule and rode out to where the cattle were and saw for himself. His next move was to ride over to White Oaks and consult Jim East, who was the man in charge of the outfit that Charlie had come with into New Mexico. East sent him back to Tularosa with orders to go by Fort Stanton and examine the hides of cattle that had been killed at the butcher shop there. Charlie did this, having noted several of the hides at the butcher shop, and then he came back to Tularosa. He stayed there with Coghlan and told Coghlan what he had found out.

Coghlan I think got suspicious of me, but he made an agreement with Siringo not to issue another of those steers on his beef contract, but to keep them until spring when Siringo's outfit might come and cut them out and take them back to the Canadian [River]. Charlie left the next morning for the Three Rivers ranch; I happened to be going into Tularosa the same day. So we met and had a good talk in which we got everything fixed up so that in case Coghlan issued any more of those cattle, we could get him tangled up in court.

On the Three Rivers ranch lived George Nesmith and his family. She did the cooking and George worked on the farm. I had told Charlie Siringo that he need not hesitate to talk to Mr. and Mrs. Nesmith about the cattle, as I and them had talked the whole thing over since I had seen him, and they would make him a star witness in the courtroom.

What took me into town that day was the need of telling old Pat that a bunch of his cattle had been stolen from Three Rivers and had been driven across the plains to the San Andres Mountains someplace. About 400 head had been taken, and the old man lost no time in getting together a bunch of men and starting them on the trail of the cattle. The trail led up Embrie [Hembrillo] Canyon, right by where Watson Ritch has his ranch now. I did not go with the crowd after the cattle, but stayed all night in Tularosa. Charlie stayed all night at the ranch at Three Rivers. He had a long talk with Mr. and Mrs. Nesmith, and they told him more than they had ever told me about the ways of old Pat.

When I returned to the ranch, Coghlan and Billy Gentry came up right behind me. It was in the spring; I couldn't say exactly when, but the grass was beginning to get green in places. Coghlan ordered me to go and help Gentry round up those steers and drive them over to Fort Stanton, and turn them in on his contract, which was in direct violation of the promise he had made to Siringo. Of course I couldn't say anything that would let Coghlan know that I had any knowledge of that promise to Charlie Siringo, and I was in a quandary what to do. But by a strange coincidence, Coghlan had brought me a letter that day from Tom Norris, in which he said, "I will get there some time in April and I will have a little money and five or six real good horses, counting your red roan, and we will get a ranch on the Peñasco."

So I felt bold enough to defy the order about the cattle. I told Coghlan that I begged to be excused as I didn't care to handle those cattle. It did not take the old man very long to fire me; he did it right away in fact. I had a little money but my private horse was over on the Rinconada. He had got away from me and wandered over there. I asked Coghlan about taking one of his horses to go and get mine, but he told me not to touch one of his horses, adding that if I wanted my horse I could go after him afoot. This made me talk back to him pretty straight. I said, "Old man, you had better not get too gay; if I have to, I will take one of your horses, whether you say so or not." And I did. I went and got a horse out of the stable, saddled him up right in front of Coghlan. He didn't say a word, but turned and went into the house. I rode on over to the Rinconada and got my horse. I sent his horse back that same evening from the [Mescalero] Agency by the buckboard.

When I got up to the Agency I mailed a letter to Tom Norris back at Camp Thomas, telling him what had happened, and saying that I was going back to Seven Rivers and work for old man McKittrick. He and I were good friends, and I was sure I could stay with him until Tom came out.[2]

Chapter 7

˖ ✦ ˖

How We Guarded One of Pat Garrett's Prisoners

In the early spring of 1881, after Pat Coghlan and I had had a tear up and I quit working for him at Three Rivers, I went over to the McKittrick Ranch at the "Jones" water hole, about 15 miles northwest from Seven Rivers. I went to work helping Mr. [Felix] McKittrick branding stock. He was a good friend of mine. Every morning he and I would get our horses after breakfast and drive up a bunch of cows and calves and brand the calves during the day. I did the heavy work, roping and tying the calves, and McKittrick would do the branding.

About the fourth day I went to work for him, as I remember it, just before noon Pat Garrett rode up with a prisoner in custody. Pat who was then sheriff of Lincoln County had a warrant [for the arrest of] H. M. Beckwith, the father of Bob Beckwith who was killed by Billy the Kid.[1] After the death of his son, the old man went sort of crazy over it. He blamed his son-in-law, W. H. Johnson, for inducing Bob Beckwith to go up to Lincoln and take part in the fight in which he was killed. One night a few weeks after the killing of Bob, old man Beckwith called Johnson to the door of the house and shot him. He had left the country after this, and the warrant that Garrett had was a year or two old before he had any chance to serve it on him.

Pat had been on the way to Rocky Arroyo to look after some horsethieves, he had received a tip they were there. When he picked up old man Beckwith between "Tar" Lake and the Gilbert ranch on the Lower Peñasco, he did not know what to do with Beckwith while he went over to Rocky Arroyo, after the bunch of horsethieves. Pat couldn't very well tell this man to go on in and get himself locked up. If he took him to Lincoln and put him in the jail there, the chances seemed good for him to be murdered by a mob. Garrett brought him by the Gilbert ranch, where we were branding calves, and left him in our care while he (Garrett) went on to Rocky Arroyo and back. Pat expected to return the next day.

As I said, the two, sheriff and prisoner, got there just before dinner. We went down and cooked a meal for the four of us. After dinner Pat said to McKittrick: "Mack, I have a prisoner. I can't take him with me and will you and John be so kind as to keep him here until tomorrow evening?"[2]

Mack said: "Yes, Beckwith can tally the calves as John and I brand them."

Beckwith, who was a highly educated man and quite a Shakespearean scholar, said, "Yes, I will be glad to help."

McKittrick told the prisoner, Beckwith, to unsaddle his mule and stake him out on a hill, where the grass was very good. He did so and helped us brand the rest of the day. When night came we went down into the chosie,[3] or dugout, had supper and talked until bedtime. McKittrick then asked Beckwith where he wanted to sleep—in the chosie or out under the brush arbor. "Mr. McKittrick," the old man said, "if it will be just the same to you, I would prefer sleeping out under the brush arbor, in order to have the advantage of the fresh air." Not a bad idea for a man under guard. "Suit yourself," answered McKittrick, "we have plenty of blankets and I can let you have a mattress."

Sometime during the night he got up, saddled his mule, and skiddaddled, vamoosed.

The afternoon of the next day Garrett came back. We were plenty nervous about how he would take the news of Beckwith's leaving. Garrett looked all around, and then said to McKittrick, "What did you do with Beckwith?"

"Why," replied McKittrick, "the darned hound left last night. We gave him the best we had; we even let him drink out of our only tea cup. But he got insulted and saddled up in the night and left." Garrett said, "Well, you have played the devil letting my prisoner get away." The only retort McKittrick made was, "The darned hound didn't know good treatment when he got it." Pat helped us brand all that evening and stayed all night with us. That night McKittrick gave Garrett the same bed Beckwith had the night before, remarking: "Now, Pat, don't you do like Beckwith did, saddle up and leave in the night without thanking us for our hospitality."

Pat replied in the dry sort of humor he possessed: "Well, Bill [*sic*], I'll just thank you now."

The man who had sworn out the warrant against Beckwith was a bitter enemy. Garrett was really afraid to take the old man back up to Lincoln and put him in the jail there for fear he would go like a one-armed Irishman who had killed Judge Stone's little boy a year or so before. The prisoner had been mobbed after being put in the Lincoln jail.[4] Garrett never had had a prisoner murdered. The feeling was still bitter between men of the opposite sides in the Lincoln County War, and Garrett knew that the warrant issued against Beckwith had been trumped up by his enemies. However, it was placed in his hands regularly to serve and he could not do otherwise than serve it.

I have always believed that down in his heart, Pat Garrett wanted that prisoner to escape from us, although that is my own personal opinion entirely. Garrett was a man who wanted justice done. We learned sometime after[ward] that Beckwith had made his way to Fort Stockton, where he stopped for awhile. He wrote Garrett a letter. I read the letter as Garrett showed it to me. The old man could sling the English and he sure spread himself in that letter. Beckwith later moved over into the Big Bend country. He got a little farm and got into a fight with Mexican neighbors over water and they killed him. I was told about this at Fort Stockton some years later.[5]

Recovering Stolen Horses from the Indians

In the early spring of 1881 I was camped with a detachment of government soldiers under command of Lieut. Van Dusen, on the head waters of the Sacramento River. We were looking for a bunch of renegade Indians who had left the Mescalero Reservation. For several days we had not had much luck. One morning the lieut. and two Indian scouts, Peso and Choneska (the latter died only a few months ago), went over into the Wills Canyon, Hay Canyon and that part of the country. Before leaving, Lieut. Van Dusen asked me if I would be afraid to take a trip over into the Rincon and see what I could find over there. The Rincon country in those days was a great hide-out for the Indians, scouting for deer, hiding stolen stock and keeping out of the way of the government soldiers. It has since been used at times for similar purposes by the "palefaces." I told the lieut. I would go over; that if I got scared out I had a good horse and could probably outrun anyone I was afraid of.

I went over into the Rincon alone, over an old Indian trail. After traveling a few miles I came to the top of a hill. Looking across a valley to what is now known as the Kid Spring (not Billy the Kid Spring, strange enough), I saw a bunch of horses over there, some 15 or 16 head. In order to inspect them closer, I worked around until I could make out the brands. The most of them were from the Seven Rivers country and several were from Old Mexico, and also among the horses were two government horses with their left ears cropped. I knew there was a $100 reward offered each for the government horses.

I returned to the Sacramento camp that night but said nothing to the lieut. about the horses. I was well aware that my job would play out as soon as we got back to the Agency. I was doing a little work in self-defense.

The next morning, the entire detachment broke camp and went to Culp Wells on the west side of the Sacramentos. We stayed there that night and the next day we went to Dog Canyon, where we camped that night. I was in advance of the company and when we got to the water I saw fresh horse tracks. I followed the trail up the canyon a distance.

I was alone and ran across three old Indians; old Nayuka and two old squaws (old Nayuka was killed at Tularosa a few years ago by being hit by a train). From where the Indians were camped on the hill they could see the soldiers coming behind me. I told the old man, who could speak excellent Spanish, that he might just as well go down and give up, as the soldiers would get him anyway. Old Nayuka took my advice, and gave up. The old man and the two squaws were there watching the horses I had seen the day before.

About all the food they had was some deer meat. The next morning old Nayuka went to the lieut. and asked for rations from the commissary. Lieut. Van Dusen had nothing but hard tack and bacon and the Indians wouldn't eat that. The next day we made it to the old Alamo ranch (about a mile south-west of the mouth of Alamo Canyon). Tom Keeney[1] was occupying the ranch then, but I think he was away at the time. The Indians still were not eating. I heard the lieut. say, "I don't know what I'll do with these damn Indians, they won't eat any thing we give them." I told him to have the cook take the rice they had, cook it up and put plenty of sugar and currants in it, and they would sure eat it.

Our scout, Choneska, saw what the cook was doing and said he bet they would eat that—and they did. They ate so much it made them sick. The lieut. was worried quite a little by those sick squaws for we certainly had no hospital unit along with us.

Our next move was to La Luz. Pat Coghlan had a quantity of fresh meat delivered there for soldiers who were on the lookout for renegade Indians. Coghlan had a beef contract with the government. Lieut. Van Dusen got some meat for his command and the Indians. We reached La Luz pretty early in the morning and we stayed there that day and the next. The morning we got there, the lieut. told me that we would be camped there for that day and the next. He gave me a book to read, so I wandered up the ditch a ways to find a quiet place to do some reading. I sat down under a big cottonwood tree. At that time there was no such thing as a wire fence in the whole country. I heard a noise, and looking up the ditch saw Tom Keeney coming with a big roll of bedding on his shoulders. Tom was reputed to be about the laziest man in the entire country, but he was sure making close to record time that morning.

He walked up in front of me, dropped his 30- or 40-pound roll of bedding on the ground. He sat down on the bedding and asked me if we had learned anything as to the whereabouts of those renegade Indians. I told him we had not rounded up any Indians except Nayuka and two old squaws, and they were in town now.

Tom said, "Nayuka, the devil, he don't amount to anything—it's the other fellows you want!"

I told him we had not found the renegades.

He said, "I know where they are right now."

I asked, "Where, Tom?"

He said, "Up there on upper La Luz Canyon, on top of the mountain."

I asked him how he knew they were there, and this was Tom's story:

Real early this morning I got ready and took that little orphan boy of mine and [my] team and buggy with bedding and some supplies and went up to that homestead of mine on the Martucha,[2] to do some assessment work.

When I got there the boy turned around with the team and came back to La Luz. I had enough grub to last for six days. I cleaned up around the place, and when noon came I went into the house to cook my dinner. I saw a shadow in the doorway and turned and there sat my old friend Comesco on the door step. Old Comesco and I had been good friends for years. I was very glad to see him. The old boy had a gun and also a bow and arrows on his back. I shook hands with him and asked him in to share my dinner with me.

He was not a bit bashful and came right in and ate his full share of the dinner. During the meal I thought I would "pick" old Comesco to see if he would tell me about the renegades then off the reservation. I asked him if he knew anything about them and he said, "Yes, I came from their camp this morning," speaking in Spanish.

I questioned him further and said, "Comesco, you and me have been friends for long time."

"Yes," he said, "you and me been friends for long years, and we always will be."

Tom thought he would go into the matter a little deeper and he said, "Comesco, if them wild people took a notion to come down here and kill your old friend, what would you do to keep them from it?"

Comesco replied, "Do you think I would let them enemies kill you? I wouldn't let your enemies kill you—they will never kill you."

Tom said, "What would you do, Comesco, to keep them from killing me?"

"Why," said Comesco, "I would come down and kill you myself, and wouldn't let your enemies do it."

Tom said to me, "John, how did I know but that was not what he was there for right then, so I rolled my bedding up and left my provisions, and got out of there damn quick."

At La Luz our guides, Peso and Choneska, quit us and went back up over the mountains to Mescalero. The next day the detachment went to Tularosa and stayed all night there. We had been carrying with only a pack outfit. The government sent a couple of wagons to meet us there.

At that time Lieut. Van Dusen was in charge of quite a bunch of soldiers at the Agency. The late Major W. H. H. Llewellyn was Agent there at the time. I was discharged as a civilian helper at Tularosa. The soldiers went on up to the

Fig. 10. J. B. "Billy" Mathews (seated) and John H.
    Riley, as employees of L. G. Murphy & Co.,
    1870s. Courtesy of the Nita Stewart Haley
    Memorial Library, Midland, Texas; Robert H.
    Mullin Collection, Photo RNM, A, 200.1.

Agency. All the Indians they could get hold of were under
sentry guard night and day. They were camped on a hillside.

After I got my pay I went back to the Rincon country. The
late Dr. Blazer cashed my check for me. I went back over there
to get those horses. I had told no one about them, not even
the lieut. I found all of them. Of course, I took a big chance
that those renegade Indians were not over in the Rincon.

I rounded up the horses and pulled for Fort Stanton. I went
over the head of the Sacramento River and followed the old
Indian trail along the summit to where Cloudcroft is now. It

was so cold I nearly froze to death as I camped out one night there. The next morning I pulled for the head of Silver Springs Canyon. I left that canyon where it enters Elk Springs Canyon. There I took an old Indian trail to White Tail Spring. I stayed all night there.

I finally made it to Fort Stanton. When I got into view of Fort Stanton late in the evening, I camped there. I got one of the two government horses, with the cropped ear, saddled him up and rode into the fort to show the commanding officer what I had.

Lieut. Clark was in command. He said, "Johnny, you are a lucky boy, there is a $100 reward on that horse." I told him I had another one. I went and got the other government horse and turned them both over to the officer. The lieut. said, "Those horses have been checked in as dead."

Most of the other horses belonged over in Seven Rivers country.

I got my money and John C. Delaney, sutler at the Fort, cashed my check.

I hit the trail back to Peñasco. There I took the trail to Seven Rivers with the balance of the horses. I stopped with Mr. McKittrick. From there I sent in word to the owners of the horses that I had them. Two belonged to Van Wyck, two to Pete Corn, and one to old man Gardner. I had 14 head when I got to Seven Rivers and found owners for most of them.

When I got to Seven Rivers there was a letter waiting for me from Tom Norris, who was then in Arizona. He said he would join me in April and he wanted me to try to get a little farm on the Peñasco where we could go to farming. When I got up on the Peñasco, I picked out a ranch that seemed just what we would want. It was owned by a man named Jim Hagen, and when I inquired of him what he wanted for it, he replied $300.

The money I got for the government horses went to purchase the farm. It was what is now called the Bryant place, right against Round Mountains on the east side of the Peñasco, about four miles from the mouth of the Elk. I asked Hagen if it would suit him to take some horses in part payment, and he said it would be all right if they were the right kind of stock. As it seemed likely the trade would go through, I stopped with Billy Mathews, who was living in that vicinity, until Tom Norris came over.[3]

* ⋆ *

Life in the Sacramentos in 1881

Tom had some bad luck at the point of the White Sands. The red roan horse that we bought at Camp Thomas got sick on the water there, and Tom had to leave him in Tularosa Canyon with a Negro named John Copeland, to let him rest up. The understanding was that I was to come and get the horse, but then when we did, the Negro claimed the horse as his own.

All this was around April '81 and it was about the same time that Alex Nunnelly and Charlie Wall had a fight with the Tularosa people over the water. The Mexicans were very much afraid of Charlie Wall because he came from Texas, but they did not fear Alex Nunnelly because he came from Arkansas. But when the fight got started, Alex proved the better fighter. He picked up his Winchester and killed five of the Mexicans—killed them himself. Another curious thing about this fight was that it took place right on the line between Doña Ana and Lincoln counties. The line was right above Cottonwood Springs then; Alex stood in Lincoln County and killed the Mexicans in Doña Ana County.[1]

Alex and Charlie went up to the Agency and sought protection there at Blazer's Mill. All this happened a few days after Tom passed on his way to the Peñasco, and when I went down to get the horse, I found these boys prisoners at the mill. They had sent word to Lincoln for Garrett to come down and get them. They thought that the safest place would be at Lincoln. The Mexicans did form a mob and try to get the boys, but the people at Blazer's Mill would not allow them to get them. The night after the killing someone—it was never known who it was although it must have been some of the Mexicans, climbed into the corral and killed my old red roan horse, thinking that he belonged to the Negro, John Copeland, and that by killing the animal he would be getting revenge, for the Negro was mixed up in the fight.

Alex and Charlie were carried up to Lincoln and put in the jail, not as prisoners, but as trusties. Kid was in jail there at the same time, and they were present when he made his escape.

But to return to my own experiences. Tom and I bought the Hagen ranch, paying some cash and some horses. We got a yoke of steers and some farming tools, which consisted chiefly of a plow and a hoe. We turned right in and put in a big crop of corn and beans. Thinking that we did not have enough land in cultivation on the place we had bought, we rented some more land from Billy Mathews, who lived on the ranch above us. Altogether that year we had about thirty acres of corn—possibly a little more.

In the summer I made a trip over to Three Rivers to visit my friends Mr. and Mrs. George Nesmith. It was Mr. and Mrs. Nesmith with their little daughter who were murdered several years later at a point below the White Sands, while they were on their way to Las Cruces.

I went over by the way of the Mescalero Agency and Tularosa. The next day after I got there, George and I were sitting out on the east side of his cottage. The south side of the valley where we were was quite level then. It was early in the afternoon. I said to George: "This thing looks kind of dangerous to me." There was a very hard storm which looked like a cloudburst and it extended over the watersheds of all three of the tributaries to Three Rivers—the Golondrina, Indian River, and the "Barber" fork. All of these tributaries flow together within a short distance of each other and when all are in flood a dangerous volume of water comes down. About two o'clock in the afternoon, just after we had eaten dinner, we looked up the valley and could see a wall of water coming which looked several feet high.

We all struck for higher ground and none too soon. Already the flood was nearly on us and coming at great speed. Mr.

Nesmith had to carry his wife through a swag^2 and we had to wade in water up to our waists. We finally got to the high ground to the north of the house and stayed for a few hours until the water went down. We were able to come back to the house before nightfall. Everything in the house had been water soaked and was covered with the muddy sediment.

I was preparing to leave the next morning. George Nesmith proposed that I take some hogs he had over to the Peñasco and feed them on shares. He said he had no feed for them and I had a corn crop that could be partly utilized in that way. The hogs fortunately enough had been up where the water did not reach.

By the way, south of where the old Coghlan residence was, an arroyo was started by that flood of 1881 which has been growing a little year by year ever since, until now it is a terrible gash in the earth. Where the [Albert B.] Fall home is now, was a cienega or marsh at that time. The arroyo drained it and that spot is now dry ground. Also, the flood caused a stream to break forth near the mouth of Three Rivers Canyon, and which is where the Hatchet ranch now gets its supply of water.

Well, I loaded those hogs into my wagon and went to my home on the Peñasco by way of Fort Stanton. When I got back to the ranch about September 1, Tom Norris had sold it for $800 to a man by the name of Bill Hunter [sic; Hinton?]. He said to me, "John, I'm going to take this money and go down on the Pecos where we can buy some cheap yearlings. Then we can go into the cattle business right up here in the mountains." We made a big corn crop, and Tom gave me all of the crop and two yoke of steers, and told me that would make me safe. Some of it [the corn] I sold to Fort Stockton [sic; probably Fort Stanton], and the rest to the cow men down on the Pecos.

He told me to go and get that Agua Chiquita ranch that Jim Dowling and John C. Delaney owned. I went there and located in some old Mexican buildings which belonged to Dowling & Delaney. I went to see Delaney at Fort Stanton and agreed to buy the buildings for $75, which was what he asked. I came on back past the Dowling Mill at Ruidoso and Mr. Dowling went his partner some better and said that I might have the old buildings over on the Agua Chiquita. By this time I was through gathering corn on the Peñasco and had sold most of it to the government. I moved the hogs and everything over to the Agua Chiquita.

Tom had taken one of his horses, and one of mine, hitched them to a wagon, and went as far as Pecos City. There he struck an old freighter from El Paso who persuaded him to go to the end of the Mexican Central Railroad, which was about 60 miles below Juarez, buy out a saloon, and get rich quick. Soon as he got down there, he bought one sure enough, and wrote back to me saying, "Sell the ranch and everything you've got. Come down to the end of the Mexican Central in Old Mexico. Do this as quick as you can. I am making all kinds of money." But I couldn't see it as he did; so I sold nothing and remained where I was.

In two or three weeks I got another letter from him, very different in tone from the other. "If you haven't sold out," it read, "for God's sake don't sell anything. They have confiscated everything I have, even to my old saddle horse. I am jumping on old Bill, and will beat them to the line before they get him, too." Sure enough, he just made it. Tom did not get back to New Mexico but landed in Abilene, Texas, and went to driving a big freighting outfit. A year or so later he married his employer's daughter and the old man made them a present of a 6-mule team. Tom worked in Texas for a number of years and reared a big family. The last time I saw him was in 1917.

My nearest neighbors on the Agua Chiquita were Sam Collins and Bud Harlin [sic; Holland?], [who] had a herd of cattle at Bluewater, ten miles from where I lived. They were working for Dowling & Delaney. Sam Collins wanted to cut some hay for the winter time, so I told them that if they would cut the hay and haul it, they could take two loads to my one. I had a big bull wagon and also agreed to furnish the steers with which to do the hauling. Where there is little grass over there now, grass grew hip high that fall. I was still busy with my crop and told Collins (he had a mowing machine) to cut the hay in Agua Chiquita Canyon. Collins agreed, so I had plenty of hay through the winter of 1881–82.

Fig. 11. Family cabin in the Sacramento Mountains, N.Mex., n.d. Probably similar to the cabins John Meadows lived in along the Agua Chiquita. Courtesy of New Mexico State University Library's Archives and Special Collections, Ms0110, Blazer Family Papers, RG81-038.

While they were cutting the hay, I did nothing but just kill meat—deer, bear, and elk.

I had turned my hogs loose to fatten on the acorns and other wild feed and the bears had gotten every last one of them by the time I finished my work on the Peñasco and moved to the Agua Chiquita. But I got sweet revenge on the bears. I killed a number of them and sold enough to pay me for the loss of the hogs. I had my headquarters all winter on the Agua Chiquita and lived in a cabin on the Andy McDonald place which had been built in the 70s.

I next joined forces with old man McGee, who had a big crop of potatoes, which he was under contract to furnish to Fort Stanton. I agreed to help him haul his potatoes over to the fort, and I managed to get over a tremendous load with those three [yokes of?] steers and a little trailer wagon. I also carried about a thousand pounds of elk, deer, and bear meat with me, which I sold along the Hondo and the Rio Bonito, and at Lincoln and Fort Stanton.

We had to make the trip in by the Feliz ranch on account of Elk Springs Canyon being full of snow. I was gone several days on this trip, and when I got back home I had a curious experience. When I left, I had among my provisions a barrel of sauerkraut, five hundred pounds of meat, a can with three or four gallons of molasses in it, and very nearly a gallon of coal oil. When I got back in the night and opened the door, I smelled a most horrible smell. The light from the snow made it possible for me to make out to see a bulk in front of me on the floor. I struck a match and lit a little lamp on the mantlepiece [*sic*]. Then I found that the pile on the floor consisted first, of my big wool mattress spread out on the floor; my meat on top of the mattress; the sauerkraut on the meat; the molasses on top of the sauerkraut; the coal oil on the sauerkraut. It was the dog-gonedest, stinkingest mess a person ever smelled.

To get rid of it, I went out again and drove the ox team a little closer. Then I took a big heavy rope, tied it to the mattress, and hauled the whole mess down on the plain some distance from the house. That was what I came back to after my first potato trip. So I evidently did not make anything on the trip.[3]

Chapter 10

⋆ ⋆

Murder of the Nesmith Family

That winter I located on [Agua] Chiquita Creek in some old cabins the Mexicans had built there years before, but had vacated on account of the Indians running in on them and killing a lot of them. I made up my mind I would stay and I did. I had now four pretty good head of horses that I had traded for, and two yokes of steers and a big bull wagon that I had got to haul corn in from a man named Fisher who came from Arkansas. I threw everything I had into this wagon and drove out to the Chiquita and located right there. I was the first white man that tried to locate on the Chiquita. The grass was extra fine all down the canyon below where Weed is now.

During the winter John W. Poe and Charlie Siringo visited me there. They wanted to know about some of Pat Coghlan's cattle deals, and I told them all I knew. They especially wanted to know about a bunch of cattle stolen over in the Texas Panhandle and driven over and sold to Coghlan. Poe was a U.S. Marshal at the time, I believe. I told the officers where to go to get the information they wanted concerning the cattle. That started a law-suit against Coghlan.

At the time, Billy the Kid was suspicioned of having something to do with this cattle deal. I told Poe and Siringo that in my honest opinion the Kid had nothing to do with that deal and that Tom Cooper was in charge of the herd when they crossed the Pecos below Fort Sumner. I knew that much. They drove that bunch of cattle by White Oaks and sold some of them to a butcher there. The rest of the cattle they drove to Three Rivers and sold them to Pat Coghlan.

Pat Coghlan bought the cattle without taking any bill of sale from Tom Cooper. The men interested in the sale were Billy Wilson, Tom Pickard [*sic;* Pickett], Charlie Bowdre and Tom Cooper, all hardened characters. They split the money. George Nesmith and his wife were witnesses to Coghlan's statement to Cooper to "bring more of the cattle" and he would buy all they would bring. He knew they were stolen over in Texas. At the time the cattle were brought in, Coghlan had a contract with the government to supply beef at Fort Stanton for the soldiers. Cooper and his gang got the pay for the cattle and returned to White Oaks. Such cattle deals as that were not infrequent in those days. "Rustling" was quite common.[1]

Court convened in April or May—April, I think [1882], and they got forty-two indictments against Coghlan for those steers. I had put Mr. Nesmith in possession of the information which he was going to use on the witness stand against Pat Coghlan when the latter was to be tried in connection with those cattle. Mr. Nesmith never got a chance to go on the witness stand.

Coghlan got a change of venue from Lincoln to Las Cruces on those forty-three [?] indictments that Charlie Siringo got against him. I went over to Lincoln at the time for court and there I met John W. Poe and Pat Garrett. They sat down and talked with me about this cow business, and I told them practically the same thing that Charlie had told. Col. Fountain was there as the prosecutor in this case, and he said about me, "He is an important witness against Coghlan."

Court convened at Las Cruces, and I had to go. I knew it would not do to leave anything in my house on the Chiquita, so I picked up all I had and took it with me in the wagon to Las Cruces. When I got there, I found George Nesmith and his wife also there, for the same purpose as I was. I had sold my steers and wagon and outfit and practically all I had, except my one-horse wagon and a team, and had between $300 and $400 with me. We had to remain four or five weeks in Las Cruces on account of court. This case against Coghlan was holding up the finishing of the term of court more than anything else. Coghlan was trying to get a new trial, and they let him have it.

The day before his case was called, he and the prosecuting attorney, Judge Newcomb, drove up to the town of
Doña Ana. The next morning Coghlan's case came up. He
was first tried for buying cattle without taking a bill of sale;
he pleaded guilty to that and was fined $150 and costs. The
prosecuting attorney then "nolled" all the rest of the cases.
Now, that summer Judge Newcomb put a good herd of cattle
on the Rinconada, and sold George N. Newell a half interest
in it.[2]

After court had adjourned, George Nesmith and his wife
and I came back to Tularosa. Of course, Coghlan had no more
use for any of us. So George and me located a ranch right
where the Hatchet ranch is now. I put up the money—George
didn't have any—and we settled right close up to old Pat.
After we got a house built for me and ten or twelve acres
fenced and plowed up, I told George and his wife, "Now, you
stay here on the ranch and take all you can make this year. I
will take my team and go to freighting."

I traded around and got me a good team. I scratched
around and got a bigger wagon from Benito Montoya. Then I
went to freighting between El Paso, La Luz, Tularosa, the
Agency, and I even made one trip to Fort Stanton. That year
I traded for a crop on the Wesley Field ranch, just above the
Round Mountain, which consisted of corn, pumpkins, beans,
and wheat. I made a bumper wheat crop that year, which was
pretty good for so small a farm. I had the wheat cut and
threshed, and then I hauled it over to Dowlin's Mill on the
Ruidoso, a distance of about twenty-four miles.

About the first of August I went down to Dowlin's Mill to
get a load of flour to haul down to the Pecos so as to get a
good price for it. The very day I started down with this flour
[August 16 or 17], George Nesmith and his wife and 2-year-
old daughter [Lucy] started from Tularosa in a lumber wagon
for Las Cruces to see Dr. Johnson and have Lucy treated for
tapeworm. That fateful day on their journey towards 'Cruces,
the Nesmiths took their noonday lunch at the Coghlan well
near the south point of the White Sands. There they met up
with two Mexicans afoot, traveling in the same direction.

Fig. 12. Dowlin's Mill in 1888, now surrounded by Ruidoso, N.Mex. Sierra Blanca in the background. Courtesy of The Historical Society for Southeast New Mexico Inc., Roswell, N.Mex., photo no. 1300.

Nesmith, being a kind and generous man, offered to take the men in and let them ride as far as he went. Along toward evening the travelers came to the Chalk Hills vicinity some 15 miles to the south of where they had eaten at noon. Nesmith told Maximo Apodaca, who was driving for him, to turn off a little ways and they would find his old camping ground. As the wagon turned off the road, the other Mexican, Ruperto Lara, who was walking behind the wagon, raised his pistol and shot Nesmith in the back of the head, and instantly turned the weapon on Mrs. Nesmith and also shot her in the head.

The two Mexicans drove the team some distance off the road but parallel, some two and a half miles, when Lara told Apodaca that he had to kill the baby as he, Lara, had killed the parents. Apodaca thereupon grabbed the little child by the feet and slapped its head against the wagon tire. Then they got on the two ponies that had been pulling the wagon and rode into Old Mexico with the $25 they had taken from the pockets of George Nesmith. Doubtless the fiends believed that they had been so cunning in their crime that they would never be found out by mortal man. Only accidentally were they eventually brought to the bar of justice.

I was over in the Pecos Valley selling flour from the Blazer Mill at the time of the murders. I got back Sept. 26th, more than a month after the crime. I recall quite distinctly: I was farming below the Blazer Mill near Mescalero. Dr. Blazer came by on his way home from Tularosa, where he had learned what details were known of the Nesmith murder and how the bodies had been found.

The Doctor related that an old miner was on his way from the Jarillas to the San Andres. He noticed a wagon sitting quite a distance off the road, which was quite an unusual thing in those days. The miner was nearly famished for water and went to the wagon in the hope that he might find a keg or jug of water. Instead he was horrified to find three dead bodies; a man, woman, and little child.

He made his way to the San Augustine ranch this side of the Organ Mountains as speedily as he could and reached there late at night with his tired burros. He told the owner of the ranch, Mr. Benj. E. Davies, of the murdered family. The next morning, the two men returned to the wagon. There was a trunk in the wagon and in it were found papers that disclosed the identity of the three people. They also found the tracks of the horses, which evidently took the direction of El Paso.

At the time of his death while Nesmith was Coghlan's foreman, he was living on my ranch at Three Rivers. I had advanced him $300 to take up this unsurveyed land and to make certain improvements. Naturally I was interested in the case [and] not only from our friendship but on account of our business relations with Nesmith. The Nesmiths were fine people.

I went to the Davies ranch to find out what I could and then went on to Las Cruces to consult Col. A. J. Fountain. Col. Fountain told me to get back on my Three Rivers ranch and hold it. This I did as soon as I could harvest my crops on the Mescalero farm. I remained there until the next year (1883), when I traded the ranch to Coghlan for cattle. I moved the cattle over to Eagle Creek and went to work for Pat Garrett and John Poe. Two years went by and no progress had been made in solving the Nesmith murder mystery.

Garrett sent me to Fort Worth, Texas, to look after some business for him. While I was on the trip, someone sent a message from Las Cruces to an acquaintance, Seeb Gray at Eagle Creek, asking as to my whereabouts. They were trying to develop some evidence in the Nesmith case, which in reality finally proved the undoing of the murderers.

The message was sent on to me in care of the First National Bank at Fort Worth. I was talking to the president of the bank when the message came and he remarked that he had a telegram for me. I answered the wire and disclosed the information sought that it was a Mrs. Tucker, sister of Geo. Maxwell, of Tularosa, who had made a certain overcoat for Geo. Nesmith, which he was believed to have had at the time of his murder. Officers had been on the lookout for the coat.

Milt Reed, a butcher of Las Cruces, went to the little hamlet of Colorado (Hatch) to buy some cattle. He was in a hut and saw a coat hanging up that attracted his curiosity. When he went back to Las Cruces, he told Deputy Sheriff Jimmie Lloyd about the coat. Lloyd immediately went to the home of the Mexican and demanded to know whose coat it was. The ranch owner readily told him that it belonged to a man by the name of Apodaca, who was irrigating down in the field. Lloyd went down and threw his gun on the fellow and arrested him. Apodaca readily admitted his crime and said that he was ready to hang, as he had "heard that baby cry ever since he killed her."

Apodaca told the officer who had been with him in that murder and that it was Ruperto Lara, then in Old Mexico. It was soon ascertained that Lara was in or near Juarez, but it involved a fine piece of detective work to get him on U.S. soil.

Jimmie Lloyd and John Walters (father of the well-known Walters family of Bent), the latter one of Nesmith's soldier comrades, agreed to try the job of getting Lara. He was found by a representative making adobes near Juarez. The man who contacted him represented that he was a horse buyer very anxious to get together a bunch of horses quickly. Lara was finally persuaded to try and get some horses. He was told that they had a good mount for him near the Santa Fe depot (El Paso) and he fell into the trap. He went hopefully enough to near the depot, when Lloyd and Walters clapped their guns and handcuffs on him. The Santa Fe Ry. Co. supplied an engine and coach to carry the prisoner to Las Cruces.

Lara strenuously denied any part or knowledge in the Nesmith murders and went to trial. His partner Apodaca had pleaded guilty. The highlight of the trial was the evidence given by the little old lady, Mrs. Tucker, who had made Geo. Nesmith's overcoat. She was asked by the prosecuting attorney if she identified the exhibit as the Nesmith coat. She stated that it appeared to be the same coat. She continued her evidence and said that if it was the same coat, the inside of the lining would contain a colored brand picture of a woman. She had cut the woman's bust in two in laying out the cloth and cutting it. The bailiff ripped open the coat and the tell-tale picture was there as Mrs. Tucker had described. The jury was therefore convinced that Apodaca's story was true.

Apodaca was sent to the penitentiary. The day he got there, he ran and jumped over some bannisters [*sic*] about 20 feet to his death. Lara was hung. Before being hung, Lara told his story, which differed from Apodaca's. The latter stated that it was agreed that when they left La Luz or soon thereafter they had agreed to murder the first outfit from which they could supply themselves with horses. Then they would flee the country.

Lara on the contrary said that he had been hired by Coghlan to do away with the Nesmith family. However, in a test before a grand jury, Lara had failed to pick Coghlan out of a group of men. Coghlan was never arrested as an accessory. There were many who believed that he was implicated. The explanation that was made by such opinion was that he was afraid that Nesmith was on his way to give evidence before the grand jury as to alleged cattle thievery on the part of Coghlan. Court was in session at the time, Judge Bristol being on the bench.

George Nesmith was one of the soldiers of the "California Column," a company of soldiers who marched from California in the '60s, and disbanded at Old Mesilla. Many of these men married native women and their descendants are numbered by the hundreds in the Southwest: such families as Lapoint, Ames, Walters, Bruce, Barncastle, and scores of others having their origin in this soldier column. At the time of his death, Nesmith was manager of Pat Coghlan's Three Rivers farm, and his reputation was excellent among all who knew him.[3]

The Nesmith Murder

Positive Identification of the Body as that of Nesmith.[4]

Mr. John P. Gray of Tularosa was in this city on Thursday on private business, and we seized the opportunity to question him on the now almost forgotten subject of the Nesmith murder. Mr. Gray was a partner of Nesmith's, and at one time it was believed that one of the bodies was that of Gray himself, and not of Nesmith.

Mr. Gray informed us that a few days since he, with the assistance of Wesley Fields and H. C. Brown of Tularosa, and another man, had taken up the bodies of the murdered family for burial beside the remains of their other child near Blazer's Mill. In his opinion there is no longer a shadow of doubt that the body is that of Nesmith himself; the accumulation of evidence being such that it is almost impossible to arrive at any other conclusion. In the first place, Gray says that there was a decayed tooth in the back of the lower jaw that he (Gray) had sometimes doctored for toothache and he now has that jawbone in his possession with the decayed tooth in it.

Again, Nesmith's upper front tooth was somewhat decayed, with a small space between the two teeth that was noticeable when he talked. This part of the skull is also in Gray's possession. Then, some years ago, Nesmith had the misfortune to break his right arm, and it had been badly set and was never quite right afterwards. The bone of this right arm, with the fracture plainly visible, is in Gray's charge, and can be seen by any properly authorized person.

Even Mr. Davies[5] is forced to admit that this weight of evidence overbalances that of the size and shape of Nesmith's boot, and is convinced, or nearly so, that the body is that of Nesmith. The boot itself, of which there was so much talk at the time of the discovery of the bodies, is still missing, and was doubtless stolen out of the grave by the guilty parties; an evidence that they lived not far from the place, and read the newspapers. The horses have never been traced, though the brands were advertised, and the mutilated blind bridle has not been found.

When questioned as to who were the murderers, Mr. Gray was very reticent, and said he preferred to say nothing till he could back up his talk by evidence, which at present he was not able to do.

Chapter 11

⋆⋆

Arresting a Murderer in 1883 in the Agua Chiquita Country

The valleys and canyons of the Sacramento Mountains were pretty well settled in the '80s, mostly by people from Texas. Some of these older settlers are living yet, but most of them have passed on and their descendants are still in the fertile canyons of the Sacramento Mountains.

These people from Texas [who came] along in the '80s were mostly a peace-loving, law-abiding people. Their coming was resented by a few who had come earlier. This opposition resulted in several feuds and killings.

There are people living in and near Alamogordo today, who as children coming to New Mexico and the Sacramento Mountains with their parents, saw desperate characters driving off their cattle right before their eyes. I can name a few, but there are descendants of victims of such outlawry and descendants of the aggressors still living, and that would be reviving old feuds.

I will relate the general facts of one arrest that came under my experience as a deputy sheriff. A "new-comer" was the victim. In the spring of 1883, I was working on a round-up at Elk Springs, a short distance from where the little village of Elk now stands. Buck Guise was in charge of the round-up. The late John Poe (of Roswell) was the sheriff at Lincoln at that time [and] accompanied by his deputy, Jim Brent, rode up to the cow camp late one evening. Sheriff Poe said: "Buck, I would like to take one of your cowpunchers with me for a

Fig. 13. Three sheriffs of Lincoln County. Left to
right: Pat F. Garrett, James Brent, and
John Poe. Photo c. 1882–1884. Courtesy
of University of New Mexico Library's
Center for Southwest Research, Marshall
Bond Collection, photo no. 000-118-0015.

short time." Buck said: "All right, John, there they are, help
yourself." Poe came up to me and asked me if I had my gun
with me. I told him I had and that it was in my bed roll.

Sheriff Poe said to me: "John, are you pretty well
acquainted with the country over around Agua Chiquita?" I
told him I knew every canyon in that country. The sheriff said:

"We have a warrant for a man over in that country who is charged with a murder. I think that he is stopping with old man Booth." Old Booth had jumped and was living on the ranch that Bill Dowling had given me several years before.

The next morning before daylight we left camp and started for the Agua Chiquita country. We got as far as Uncle Joe Curtis' ranch on the Upper Peñasco. We stopped and Sheriff Poe asked Uncle Joe if we could get some breakfast with him. Mr. Curtis, in the spirit of all the old timers and pioneers of that day, said, "Sure, you can. There's a haystack, let your horses eat, too."

We got breakfast and pulled out up over the Gradesser Hill to the top. After we got over the hill, we hit an old Indian trail that took us direct to the Booth place. We had reason, as I stated before, to believe that the man wanted for murder was at the Booth place. When we got almost there, old man Booth stepped out into the open without his gun. However, his son Mike (later hung over in Arizona for murder) picked up a gun, sat down on a log, and held the gun across his knee.

Sheriff Poe asked Mr. Booth about Sutton, the man whom we had a warrant for on account of [his] being an alleged murderer. Booth was rather impudent in his answer, and said that he didn't know where Sutton was and wouldn't tell the officers if he did. Mr. Poe said, "Maybe he is in your house right now, and I'm going to see." Poe got off his horse and went through all four rooms of the house while Brent and I was on guard outside with our guns all ready to use at a second's warning of any trouble.

The sheriff soon came out and said that Sutton wasn't inside. I told the other men I knew of another cabin up the canyon and we started up there. Of course, we knew very well that the Booth family knew exactly where Sutton was.

After going a hundred yards or so, we saw a man up on the side of the mountain. The sheriff said that we would go and investigate who he was. The three of us started up toward the fellow riding three abreast, with the sheriff in the middle. There was a big log between us and the man, who had taken a position behind the log.

The sheriff shouted: "I believe that you are Sutton and we have a warrant for you." The fellow readily acknowledged to being Sutton and demanded that the warrant be read to him. The sheriff hesitated for a moment or two and then called on the man to drop his gun, which he did, as he saw he was outnumbered. Poe read the warrant while Jimmie Brent and I had the fellow practically covered. Poe called upon him to come out from behind the log and surrender, which he did.

We took him as far as the Booth place. When we got there, the sheriff asked him how he was fixed for a horse and saddle. The prisoner said that he didn't have one and that the sheriff would have to supply him with a horse and saddle. The sheriff said that walking was good and that the officers had plenty of time. The outcome of the matter was that the Booths furnished their friend Sutton with a horse and saddle.

After we got to where the officers had picked me up at the round-up, I stayed and went back to work. Poe and Brent took Sutton on over to the Lincoln jail. Sutton was put under a $5000 bond. Elliot Keene, a stockman, and several others went on his bond, which he jumped and disappeared for good. He had been guilty of a cold-blooded murder, committed near the mouth of the James Canyon. Payment of his part of the Sutton bond financially broke Elliot Keene. He died soon after and his widow and a number of children were left in a pitiable condition.[1]

* * *

My Association with Pat F. Garrett

I have often been asked to tell something of my asso- ciation with Pat F. Garrett, who was one of the well known characters of the Southwest in the '80s, '90s, and the first decade of the present century. Of course Garrett's most famous exploit was the slaying, as an officer, of that glamorous character, Billy the Kid, at the home of Pete Maxwell at Fort Sumner.

I first met Pat Garrett at the McKenzie Lake (Texas), near the little town of Benjamin, which did not exist then.[1] I stayed all night at his buffalo camp in the winter of 1877–78. I was on my way to Uncle George Knox's buffalo camp. I knew Uncle George Knox and felt sure that I could get a job there. In the morning, the men at the Garrett camp directed me to the Knox camp, about ten miles distant. Garrett and his partner, a man named Glenn, were both in the camp that night.

I went on to the Knox camp and got there about noon. Uncle George came out to meet me and shake hands. He asked me to get down off my horse and he treated me with genuine pioneer hospitality. He said: "Johnny, it looks like we are about through with the buffalo. There seems to be few left." He asked me if I had seen any buffalo further north as I came down. I told him I saw very few. I unsaddled and picketed my horse. Uncle George said: "Johnny, there is your old gun. I will give you ten cents apiece for every buffalo you kill."

I took the gun the next morning and went out. The most buffalo I could kill was from 8 to 12 per day—not much money for me. I had to give up hunting buffalo. I had been in the Knox camp four or five days. One morning one of Garrett's men drove in early. He had a pair of little mules hitched to a wagon. He told Mr. Knox that he wanted Knox and his men to go over to the Garrett camp, as Garrett had shot and killed his partner that morning.

Uncle George questioned the man closely as to how the killing took place. As I remember, this was about his story: Garrett and his partner fell out over a rather trivial matter. The partner, Glenn, made at Garrett with an ax. Garrett could do nothing else but retreat. He ran around the tent. His old buffalo gun was laying with the butt sticking out below the tent. Garrett grabbed the gun up and called to Glenn: "Glenn, you stop where you are or I'll kill you." Glenn, ripping out an oath, came on threateningly to kill Garrett. The latter blazed away with the old buffalo gun at close range and killed Glenn instantly. Glenn fell back into the fireplace and the boys had to drag him out.[2]

When Uncle George Knox went over [to] the Garrett camp, he took his own team. He called all the witnesses up to hear their stories. Uncle George told Garrett that the best thing he could do was to go to Fort Griffin and give himself up. He told him he believed that it was justifiable homicide, and a jury's verdict would undoubtedly be to that effect. He advised Garrett to leave the cook in charge of the camp and take all of his other men. Garrett had a large quantity of buffalo hides on hand at the time. In place of leaving anyone in camp, as Knox advised, Garrett took every man with him to Fort Griffin. There he gave [himself] up to the officers. The justice at the time, as I remember, was Jim Browning, a brother of Joe Browning who lived in Alamogordo for a number of years. Garrett was turned loose without bond and permitted to go to his camp.

While Garrett and his men were in Fort Griffin, the Knox men were camped at "Long Holes" (watering places), and we had a call from a band of Comanche Indians. They attempted to raid some of our stock about daylight one morning. We boys got out with our guns and scared the Indians away, saving Uncle George's 6-mule team that they were after.

The Indians prowled around and struck the Garrett camp. They cut up all the hides, slitting each hide into four pieces;

drove off the horses, burned the tent, and played the devil generally, partly for pure revenge against the palefaces. When Garrett got back and saw the situation, he was in somewhat of a quandary. He owed the men for skinning the hides off the buffaloes. There was not much left of any value. But he told the boys that they would take what was left down to Fort Griffin, sell it, and he would divide the proceeds among them. They did that very thing, except the men thought that Garrett had played so fair with them that they insisted that he be cut in on an equal share of the proceeds. So they divided in equal parts all around.

The next [time] I met Garrett was about two years later at Fort Sumner, early in 1880. He didn't know me and I didn't make myself known to him. Garrett was deputy sheriff at Fort Sumner. I met him a few times between then and several months later, when I left for Arizona. I still had not mentioned to him that I had ever met him before, or that I knew anything about his Lake McKenzie trouble.

I talked with Garrett and asked him if he knew where John Selman was (Selman had left Texas of necessity). Garrett said: "No, I don't know where John Selman is, and damn him I don't want to know anything about him." Selman had caused me lots of grief and if I had run across him, I might have thought it necessary for my own safety to have killed him.

At this time (spring of 1880), at Fort Sumner, Billy the Kid was on his good behavior. He was going where he pleased and was not on the dodge. I saw Garrett meet the kid occasionally, while I was laid up ill at Fort Sumner for a short time.

The particular reason Garrett did not recognize me was that I had changed my name on coming to New Mexico, for what I then thought was a very good reason. It may be that Garrett thought he had seen me somewhere before, but he didn't intimate that he did.

I had worked a short time for John Laran and John Selman, two of the hardest characters I ever saw. And as to this, there are three men who knew Selman, now living in Alamogordo today. They will tell you much the same thing, I am certain. Laran and Selman knew that I was aware of some of their crookedness and thievery. They had tried to get me thrown into jail on a trumped up charge, and if they could have done so, they would have had me murdered as they did several others. I thought best to change my name to Gray for awhile to escape any hired killers they might send after me. When I arrived at Fort Sumner, Garrett didn't recognize the name.

Later I worked for Pat Garrett and the late John Poe, of Roswell, for several years. I gave them the name of "Gray" and drew my pay under that name. A rather amusing situation arose. Mr. Garrett's mother's maiden name was Elizabeth Gray. She came from my country [county?] in Alabama. Mr. Garrett was quite sure I was a relative of his. This would have been a natural presumption, had I been giving my right name.

Finally I thought [it] best to tell Mr. Garrett the situation. In the winter of 1884–5, while working some cattle for Poe, I accidentally broke a cow's neck in roping her. Poe got mad and let me go. Pat Garrett said, "Never mind, John, I have a better job for you." I didn't want to deceive Garrett any longer as he had been such a good friend to me. So I told him the whole story as to why I had changed my name. He knew the Laran-Selman outfit and knew that a young fellow, as I was, had done pretty well in escaping from their clutches if they were after him. Each had the reputation of having killed several men. They had tried to get me when I left their crooked outfit and went to work for the Millett bros. in 1878.

Garrett said, "I am sure there is nothing on the records back in Texas against you." Laran & Selman had tried to get me indicted. Pat Garrett gave me a job that took me back across the plains to Albany, Texas. As he predicted, there was nothing against me on the records. I stayed with Luke McCabe, who was the sheriff's office deputy. He treated me royally. I came back to New Mexico, assumed my own name and went to work for the VV outfit under Pat Garrett, who was the ranch foreman.[3] I worked for about a year on the VV Ranch. And right here let me say that Garrett and I were always friends, to the very last time I saw him, a short time before his untimely death.

We were both discharged from the VV company together, and never knew the reason. We each had some cattle and Pat

Fig. 14. Angus VV Ranch, Lincoln County, N.Mex., c. 1888. Photo by
J. R. Riddle. Courtesy of the Museum of New Mexico,
neg. no. 76,148.

Garrett wanted me to gather his cattle and mine and move
them over to the plains east of Roswell. There was a great
deal of loco weed in that section and I told Garrett I was
afraid to put the cattle over there. Nevertheless, Garrett
went ahead and put his stock there—horses and cattle—and
he lost heavily of both.

I tried to hold my cattle on the White Mountain range, but
Kirby & Cree, owners of the VV outfit, made it so disagreeable for me that I had to move my stock out. I moved them to
the Tularosa section from the Rio Bonita. About that time,
John Good moved a herd of cattle in from Texas. He tried to
be pretty hard boiled and overbearing. The old man could not
bulldoze the earlier settlers out of the country, so he drifted
over into the Deming country in the course of several years.

While in the country, the Good and Cooper factions of
cowmen had a merry little war. A cowman by the name of
George McDonald was ambushed and killed up at Coyote, 8
miles northeast of Tularosa. Good was accused of being behind
that murder. It may be that no one now living can tell who committed that murder.[4] There was considerable evidence that

two men, hired killers, committed the act and left the country at once, one going east and the other west. The man going east stopped at the Andy Wilson's store the same evening McDonald was killed, to get provisions. Good was pretty definitely linked up as [an] accessory in the Howe murder case.

Garrett moved down to Uvalde, Texas, and we were not together again until 1893.[5]

Chapter 13

The Howe Murder Case

In the late eighties a man by the name of [A. H.] Howe kept a small store near where Bent now stands, just below the [Mescalero] Reservation. One night in April 1887 [June 1886] two men came to the back door of his store. Howe thought that they were Negroes as they had black faces.

They knocked on the door and the old man opened it. Without any other preliminaries, one of the men shouted: "Throw up your hands, we have come to rob you." Howe, being a powerful man around 200 pounds, hauled off and struck the man nearest to him and then slammed the door to get his gun. The other man, who had stood behind, shot through the door, the bullet going through Howe's chest. Howe picked up his shot gun and took a shot at the men, who were making for their horses, tied a short distance away. He hit one of the men, who staggered but was able to hold to his horse.

An aged Mexican by [the] name of Victorio Duran lived near by and he heard Howe calling for help and responded. Also, another neighbor, Dave Easton, heard the man calling and went over. Easton sent Victorio to Blazer's Mill for help. With a number of others I went to the scene. I got my horse out of the Blazer corral and rode down to the Howe store, being the second one there from the reservation. Sam Miller also came and remained for several hours.

I told Victorio to go to the camps of the Mescalero Indians Peso and Soch Domingo, as I wanted them on the trail, for they were good trailers and I knew them very well. They soon came and brought along "Comanche John," a somewhat noted character in those days. They all three were ready to take the trail.

I found that Howe had been dangerously wounded in the breast. Dr. Thompson soon arrived from the Blazer Mill and did what he could professionally to ease the man's dying moments. Dr. Thompson told me to take the bandits' trail and not let any people obliterate it. We used all precaution in taking their trail. They had abandoned their horses in a short distance, the horses being from the John Good outfit, which ran stock in the valley.

We crossed over a hill and canyon or two and came upon the bandit who was wounded, and the horses. We called to him to throw up his hands and he put up one hand, being unable to raise the other arm. I had work to keep the three Apaches from shooting the fellow, for according to their code he deserved shooting, and also they did not want to take any chances.

The man proved to be a young fellow quite well known in the section as "Dutchy." We took him back to the store where old man Howe was shot. We asked him to tell who was with him but he would not give us any information. Within a short time old man John Good himself rode up. He suggested that we let him talk privately with the man as he believed that he could get him to talk. I told old man Good never to mind, we would find out in time.

With the three Indians, as soon next morning as we could, we again picked up the trail where we left off. The other bandit had presumably started on afoot, and we soon found the trail. After following it for about a thousand yards, we ran onto a pair of abandoned leggings which had belonged to Walter Good [son of John Good]. We followed the trail westerly for five or six miles. We came to a high cliff that the man could not go down and he had turned south. All we had to trail him by was now and then the imprint of his boot with brass tacks in the sole. We trailed him to where he crossed the Tularosa Creek. There he apparently had stopped and attempted to wash the smut off his hands and face. We trailed him to the main road and there he had caught a ride.

Fig. 15. Camp of Chief Nulgita, Mescalero Apache Reservation, c. 1880s. Courtesy of New Mexico State University Library's Archives and Special Collections, Ms0110, Blazer Family Papers, 7.3-16.

While we were standing there for a brief rest and wondering who he had gotten a ride with, a native by the name of Molina drove up and asked us what we were looking for. We told him of the shooting, which was the first he had heard of the matter. He then told us that where we were standing was where a fellow known as "Fatty" Johnson got in with him and rode to the mouth of the Tularosa Canyon, east of Tularosa.

For certain reasons I told the Indians not to tell anyone what we had learned. In a short time a posse behind us brought us horses. Molino told us where the bandit Johnson had stopped and had gone into a Mexican camp. We went there and a Mexican, Pancho Saiz, told us our man had left only about an hour before and had taken the old government road to La Luz, which ran close to the foothills.

The Indians and I trailed the man to north of La Luz on the Sabinetto Flats, where he again quit the road and got into a hack with Walter Good, who we learned had been over to Tularosa, apparently to find out what he could about the outcome of the enterprise of robbing old man Howe. On his way back to La Luz he had picked up Johnson and learned that the thing had ended disastrously.

That morning before we took the trail, I sent a man by the name of José Telles across to La Luz by the Indian trail across the foothills, with a description of the horses. When the Indians and I got to La Luz, Humphrey Hill, who was justice of the peace there, got some help and when Johnson got out of the Walter Good hack, we arrested him. I demanded the prisoner. About that time, Billy Gentry, the constable, came up. We told him that we wanted to make sure that the man was taken back to the Agency. We put a guard of several men over him that night. We were approached by Walter Good with a bribe to turn Johnson loose. We did not dare to trust the Indians alone with him for fear they would kill him.

The next morning after daylight, while the others were eating breakfast, I was on guard alone for a short while. Johnson said to me: "John, I believe that you will tell me the truth. Is the Dutchman (his partner in the crime) killed or not?" I told him that he was not when I left. He said: "I picked him up after he was shot; shook him, and was sure that he was dead. This is the second time I have committed this sort of an act, once in Kansas, and this time I guess the end of a sea-grass rope will settle it!"

We hired Florencio Luna to take Johnson to the Agency, we serving as a sort of military escort. He had little chance of getting away alive with those three Apaches watching every move. When we got to Mescalero, Sheriff J. R. Brent of Lincoln County (all this part of the country was in Lincoln County then) was on hand. We turned the prisoner over to him. Johnson was a hard character. He asked to speak with me before he left. His request was that I be there the day he was hung and give him a big drink of whiskey. Sheriff Brent said: "Never mind, I will give you all the whiskey you want on the day you hang."

He was later duly convicted and hung at Lincoln.[1] Strangely enough, the boy "Dutchy," who was so badly shot, finally recovered. He was convicted of the crime, but got off lighter than his companion for some reason. He was sent up for seven years. About the time that he was released from the pen, George Harold, a well-known peace officer of the frontier days, and I were in El Paso trying to get a fellow for whom we had papers across the river from Juarez. We were walking up an El Paso street waiting for dark to do our work, when a young fellow stepped up behind me and said: "Johnny, don't you know me; I'm 'Dutchy.' I owe my life to you for those Indians would sure have killed me." The fellow went into Old Mexico and for all I ever heard, never came out.

The old storekeeper died early the next morning, soon after we had taken the trail.[2]

* *
*

The Cowboys and Their Diversions

In the olden days the cowboys had to have some diversion and sometimes their play was a little rough and pranky. In those days there were not so many drugstores to hang around, but they had the pool halls and the saloons and gambling joints in most every little town. Card playing, including the great American game of poker, was one of the chief amusements.

However, poker-playing was not allowed as a general practice around the headquarters, for it was a general belief that "cows and cards" didn't mix very well. The boys who liked to play poker, however, found plenty of places to get rid of any change that was burning holes in their pockets.

It was sometime about 1886, as I remember. Just before Christmas I got a letter from Pat Garrett, who was living over south of Roswell, and I was up on Eagle Creek north of Ruidoso. Pat said they were going to have a big dance at his place on Christmas day, and he wanted me to come over and play the fiddle for them. I liked to fiddle and often went to dances and fiddled all night.

I first thought that I hardly wanted to get my horse and go over a hundred miles to a dance. But I finally thought what a good friend Garrett was to me, so I decided to go. I got my old pony and it took me almost three days to get there. I arrived several days before Christmas.

An old friend of mine, A. K. Dale, who was working for Garrett, was quite a joker. It was he and McKittrick who had double-loaded the old gun for the boys to shoot the candle

Fig. 16. Pat Garrett's home east of Roswell, N.Mex., n.d. Courtesy of
The Historical Society for Southeast New Mexico Inc., Roswell,
N.Mex., photo no. 1363.

out. It like to busted the fellow's shoulder who shot off the old gun.[1]

The next morning after I got to Garrett's place, Dale asked me how I was fixed for money. I said: "Dale, I haven't but three dollars to save my soul, and can't charge Pat Garrett anything for playin' the fiddle, and I don't intend to." Dale said, "Well, we will have to start some enterprise and get some money for Christmas. I haven't a cent." The trick we tried to pull was about the meanest I ever tried to put over a fellow man.

We talked over several plans and finally Dale told me about a lone wolf that had been destroying lots of stock in the Roswell cow country. The stockmen had pooled on a reward of $100 to anyone who would bring in the scalp of that wolf. Dale told me that the animal had been seen quite often, nearly always when he was running from one tule [cattail] patch to another along the bottoms.

Dale said he knew where he could get a good buffalo gun and I told him that if he could get one, I could shoot the wolf if I could get a glimpse of him. He got the gun all right, I think he got it of Mr. Ballard, father of Charlie Ballard. We had eight or ten cartridges for it. He and I walked most of the time for two days to run on to that wolf or to get a glimpse of him. Everybody had seen it apparently but us.

Dale was suddenly seized with an idea and we changed plans. He thought it would be a brilliant idea to substitute Jim Miller's old dog for the wolf and take his scalp in. The old dog stayed at Ballard's place as much as at Miller's. He was white, but his head closely resembled a wolf's quite strangely as to color and shape. We found the poor old dog at Ballard's. He was old and worthless; Dale saw Ballard and had some sort of understanding with him about the dog.

We took the dog up on the Hondo, killed him and skinned his head and took the scalp down to Pat Garrett's place. Pat and all of the men congratulated us on getting the big bad wolf. The next morning we took the scalp and tacked it on the side of the wagon, hitched up a pair of mules, and pulled out for Roswell to show some of the cowmen what hunters we were and of course to claim our reward. We were running some chance all the time, lest someone reported seeing the real wolf still at large.

When we got to the road leading to the Miller home, we turned up that way to show the head of the alleged wolf to Mr. Miller. Mrs. Miller came out of the house with a baby in arms to see the wolf head. She said, "Many and many a time I have seen those ears bobbin' through that alfalfa patch there." I felt sorry for Mrs. Miller and to tell the truth, rather ashamed. I was about half sorry we were in the midst of a pretty raw joke. Mrs. Miller, of course, was looking at the head of her own dog and not any wolf, and she was completely fooled. Mr. Miller was away from home. Maybe he would have seen the hoax had he been there.

Leaving there, we went to Roswell. At that time there was only one saloon in Roswell and we drove up in front of it. It was full of cowboys in to spend Christmas vacation. Capt. J. C. Lea was standing out in front. He looked at the scalp and said, "Boys, you sure got him." He scratched a few lines and said, "Here's my check for my share of the reward and I am glad to pay it to you."

About the time Capt. Lea gave his check to us, Dale and I saw Pat Garrett coming riding on a lope. In place of coming to the saloon where we were, he went to the home of Phelps White. Ballard had given the thing away to Pat, and he went to Phelps White and told him not to pay us anything until we took an oath that we had part of the wolf hide. Of course we couldn't do that, and Garrett had us cornered pretty neatly.

Dale put on a bold front and feigned quite a little indignation that they had doubted us—said he, they could see for themselves. Mr. White said, "Well, boys, it's just a business transaction in a business way, that's all." By that time Col. Milne, who was another cowman, had his check made out but he hadn't given it to us yet. Dale had already cashed the Lea check and partly spent the proceeds for whiskey.

After Dale had put up the big talk for the rest of the reward and failed to get it, he jumped into the wagon and said, "Drive on, John, we can't get the rest of our money, and they can't have any of our whiskey."

Someone said, "Boys, you haven't given Capt. Lea his money back." Capt. Lea, who was certainly a good sport, said, "Let the damn rascals go with it—they are welcome to it." His check was for $20.

We went back to the Garrett ranch and treated the boys. Everyone who took a drink raised his glass and said, "Here's to the wolf." Nothing much was said about the matter any more. But Pat Garrett often twitted me about what a great wolf hunter I was. And, to tell the truth, I have never been proud of the stunt Dale and I pulled.

I played the fiddle all that night at Pat Garrett's dance on the old J. S. Chisum ranch at what is now the South Springs ranch. I rested up for a couple of days after at the Garrett home, where I always felt at home and was made welcome, and then went to my place on Eagle Creek. The wolf we hunted and didn't get was killed not long after.[2]

⋆ ⋆ ⋆

Experiences in the Early 1890s

Early in January 1892, Dave Sutherland of La Luz got me a job at the Mescalero Agency, under Col. Rhodes (father of the late Eugene Manlove Rhodes), who was then agent at the reservation. All was well with me, but in Washington they had received a complaint which was on file soon after I took the job. I believe I was born too far south to suit them there at that time. I was let out in about a month.

During the time that I worked at Mescalero, a bunch of Indians had a big fight among themselves at Trias Springs, on the east side of the reservation. An Indian by the name of "Crook Neck" was in the fight. He stated that the first shot was fired by an Indian named Charley Wyeth, who shot at "Crook Neck," who fell as though he had been killed and feigned death. Crook Neck's sister saw him fall. She was on horseback on the trail up the canyon. The fight then opened up in a big way. An Indian by the name of Jimmy Dolan shot Wyeth and killed him. Someone killed Patos Chiquito, another Indian—Chiquito was a brother of Chief Nutsalia.[1] American employees at the Agency called the chief "Old Nutty," for short.

Patos Chiquito was stabbed to death with a butcher knife. A sister of Magoosta was also killed in the brawling. The trouble was caused from the fact that the Indians had made a barrel of "Tiswin" and had also gotten hold of a lot of rotten whiskey from a bootlegger and spiked the tiswin good and strong with the bad alcohol. The mixture had set a lot of them plumb crazy, apparently. Another Indian besides the ones I

Fig. 17. Mescalero Apache Agency, N.Mex., looking southeast. Probably soon after construction of the agency buildings in 1882–1883. Courtesy of New Mexico State University Library's Archives and Special Collections, Ms0110, Blazer Family Papers, 7.7-8.

mentioned above was killed, but I don't remember his name. He was some kin of old Nobeska, a La Pan [*sic;*Lipan] Indian.

As soon as "Crook Neck" could safely rise, after he had feigned death, he started for the Agency and at the same time his sister also started on horseback, but he beat her in to the Agency. He must have been quite nimble-footed. He and his sister told what they knew of the fight.[2]

Col. Rhodes ordered out all of the police, 22 Indians, one-half of whom were Mescaleros and one-half La Pans. Steve Utter, an American, was captain of the police. Col. Rhodes came to me and said, "John, I want you to go with Steve over to Trias Springs and help him with his duties."

Steve and his 22 Indian policemen and I started. Snow was on the ground and it was pretty cold weather. Among the police was a Mescalero Indian named "Peso." (Peso died only a short time ago; we were friends for many years. I trusted Peso always.) The only reason Peso was not chief of the tribes was on account of the late Major W. H. H. Llewellyn, who was agent for several years previous to that time. Chief San Juan Grande died during the Llewellyn regime (that was back in the '80s). That left the chief-ship to be filled. The major insisted that Peso and Nutsalia decide who should succeed San Juan Grande by ballot, all the same Americano style. This was done and Peso was beaten and he and "Nutty" became bitter enemies. The major may have used some of his election technique that early in his New Mexico residency.

We rode up to Chief Nutsalia's camp just a little before sundown. All the Indians were in a surly mood, including most of the policemen. Peso wanted to kill "Nutty," his enemy and rival at the election. Steve called for the chief. The old boy came out and asked in excellent Spanish, "What do you gentlemen want?" Peso answered in Spanish, calling him an ugly name.

Fortunately, the chief came out without a gun. If he had possessed one, it is certain Peso would have killed him instantly. At the instant, every Indian policeman was off his horse and on the ground with his gun in his hand. Then they began to talk Apache. Utter and I could not *sabe* what they were saying. I said to Steve, "Make these Indians talk Spanish, Steve, so we can understand them." I was on the ground myself, between two big rocks. Steve was on his horse. The Indians reverted to Spanish and then we could tell what they were quarreling about.

For a time it looked as if there was going to be a big fight pulled off regardless of anything Steve and I could do. Finally Steve persuaded them to parley and he made arrangements for Nutsalia's outfit to be at the Agency early the next morning. A sort of truce was arranged and Steve asked Chief Nutsalia where the dead Indians could be found. The chief detailed an Indian to show us where the fallen Indians were. Three of them were in a bunch in an arroyo, where a bed had been made for them out of pine boughs.

Steve sent four policemen to look up the horses belonging to the dead people. Their orders were to take good care of the horses and not to let them be killed. It was the custom to bury all of a dead Indian's personal property with him, and kill his horses right by his grave, so that he would be well out-fitted in the "Happy Hunting Grounds."

The next morning Chief Nutsalia got his outfit together as he agreed and started for the Agency. No one was arrested and the matter was dropped. There was some bitterness between the Mescalero Apaches and the La Pan Apaches, which cropped out if they got to drinking. In the fight above related, the "honors" were even—there were two dead Mescaleros and two dead La Pans.

Later on Jimmy Dolan, who had [line missing] murdered on the reservation. Joe Tria, another Indian, was found killed in the same manner, as was also an Indian named W. H. H. Llewellyn (named after Major Llewellyn).

As I said before, I worked only a month when Col. Rhodes had to let me out on orders from Washington.[3] I hitched up my team and with [my] household goods went over to where my brother-in-law, Mel Lusk, lived on the Agua Chiquita, in the Sacramento Mountains. After I got my wife and step-daughter settled there, I took my team and went down to "Eddy," now Carlsbad, to work at what I could find to do. The first work I got there was from W. H. (Bud) Woods, now of Alamogordo, who has lived here since the beginning of the town. Mr. Woods at that time was one of the stalwarts of the Eddy Bros.' activities in the Eddy section.

After I got through with his work, Mr. Woods got me a job with Trimble Bros. up on the big flume. I did anything I could find to do and between several friends I had work most of the time, and made a little money. I got to Carlsbad (or Eddy) about the first of April, 1892. About the first of June I wanted to put my daughter in school and made a trip back up to the Agua Chiquita and back. I took supplies to the family and brought my daughter back down to Eddy and placed her in school.

I worked on the Eddy Bros.' projects until fall—I worked for contractors. I was not aware that Cupid was so busy, but a young man, Walter Trimble, came to me and said that he and my stepdaughter were planning to get married. I tried to talk the young lady into keeping at school for awhile, but I didn't make any progress in that direction. So I told them that

Fig. 18. Notzili (Nutsalia), Mescalero Apache
leader of the Elk Springs area, c. 1880s.
The lance, shield, and possibly clothing are
photographer's props. Courtesy of New
Mexico State University Library's Archives
and Special Collections, Ms0110, Blazer
Family Papers, 7.7-56.

positively Callie would have to go and talk the matter over
with her mother, and that I would take her up to see her
mother. I told the young man that he would have to marry the
girl at her mother's home, if they were to be married. He was
pretty sure they could talk the mother into the notion of letting them get married, and young Trimble brought along
Parson George [Gage] and he married them.[4]

After my stepdaughter got married and went back to Eddy, my wife also went down there. She rented a restaurant. During the time I lived there, I was working for the P. I. & I. Co., doing some riprapping.[5] One Saturday evening I was going up to get my pay check cashed and met a friend. He said, "Johnny, haven't you a good lot of money in the bank up there?" I told him that all I had was in the bank. He told me to get all I had out as quickly as I could. I asked him what was wrong. He said to never mind about that but to just go and call for my money. I asked the cashier to cash my check and also that I wanted all of my money. His name was Brown. He asked me who had been talking to me. I said no one had told me anything, which was quite true.

I got my money, about $200, and put it in Jake Owen's safe up at the livery stable. The bank cashier went to the penitentiary in due time for being too careless of other people's money. Some of his associates should have gone also, but did not.[6]

I stayed the rest of 1892 and up to April 1893 in Eddy. Then [my] wife and I came back to La Luz. I made a deal with the Trujillo estate administrator for forty acres of land and three water rights. Later on, José Torres contested title to the land and won it. In June 1893 my wife died and rests in the La Luz cemetery. There is a little plot of ground I own next to her grave, and very soon I will be asleep by her side.

I took all of my household goods—everything I had, and took them over to Eddy to give [to] my stepdaughter, Mrs. Trimble. Her husband was wanting to go back to Mason county, Texas, where he had a home. About this time, I got a letter from Pat F. Garrett, who was at Uvalde, Texas. He had heard of my misfortune and wrote me to come down there, as a big company was preparing to put in a big dam and irrigation works on the Nueces River.[7]

I left for Uvalde. I took the Trimbles' household goods to where they desired to stop. I got to Pat Garrett's ranch in late November or early December. I stayed until February, 1894, waiting for the big project to open up. I got discouraged at the looks of things and sold two of my horses and came back towards New Mexico in the early spring. I got as far as Old

Fort Stockton, which had become an abandoned post. I had been there about 20 years before when things were humming.

I stopped and looked the old place over and while there I got acquainted with a man named Andy Royal. His family and mine had been old neighbors back in Alabama. He was sheriff of the county and wanted me to go to the Leon Water Holes, eight miles east, put in a crop of corn, and he would give me all I could make. He wanted to improve the land.

I put in a big crop of corn. After I got my corn laid by, work was scarce and Sheriff Royal suggested that I come over to Fort Stockton and he would give me a deputyship and I could earn some money. I told him I would come over as soon as I could get my farm work in shape. Before I did get over, the [Texas] Rangers and the sheriff and his men had picked up a man by the name of Victor Ochoa, wanted in Old Mexico, and for whose capture there was a big reward offered. I got to Fort Stockton in the evening and Mr. Royal's jailor was on a big drunk. The sheriff asked me to stay at the jail that night. I agreed. That night, Mexicans made a raid on the jail, held me up, and released Ochoa.

I served a short time as deputy. It was not long before an election was to be held. Mr. Royal had strong competition. He sort of lost his head over it and got rather ugly. He beat several of his political enemies up. In a few days after I went in as deputy sheriff, George Scarborough, a well-known peace officer and U.S. marshal of that period, came down to investigate the escape of Ochoa. He went back to El Paso and swore out warrants for the entire sheriff's force at Fort Stockton.

The day he got back to Fort Stockton and made the arrests, I was just after a bunch of horses over in the Glass Mountains. I got to the Leon Water Holes in the night. Uncle Joe Matthews, one of Sheriff Royal's tenants, said, "Johnny, they have Royal in jail and all of Scarborough's men and the Rangers were here after you." I said they will get me just as soon as Mrs. Matthews can give me something to eat and I can get to Fort Stockton. I got in to Fort Stockton after midnight. I went right to the jail. They had the sheriff, county judge, county clerk and some others all locked up for different offenses.

I went and woke up George Scarborough myself. He asked who it was. I told him and he said, "sit down and I will attend to your case when daylight comes." I was not put in jail. The J. P. was on a drunk and was not in condition to hear any complaints. Scarborough and his men had to take us to Del Rio, over 200 miles away. And that was a tedious journey in those days. We gave bond. Uncle Billy Young, a merchant of Fort Stockton, tried to get Scarborough not to take me. I figured that Scarborough got so much a prisoner and so I had to go. Mr. Young went down and he went on my bond.[8]

Chapter 16

⋆ ⋆ ⋆

Feud Murder on the Sacramento River

Ever since the palefaces came, there has been more or less rivalry for range and water in this Southwestern country. The latest phase of this human desire may be seen in the struggles under the Taylor Grazing Administration.[1] And, owing to the limits of good grazing land and watering places, all cannot be satisfied.

In the early days, some of these contests for range and water resulted either in feuds or killings, or both. I will relate some of the particulars of the slaying of Mr. C. F. Hilton, near his place on the Sacramento River (now known as the "Headquarters" ranch), by a man named James B. Smith.[2] This was entirely a needless murder and developed a great deal of hard feeling, which I dare say has not entirely disappeared until this day.

In the winter between 1893 and 1894 I was constable in the little village of La Luz.[3] And by the way, this is a spot I have always loved since I first knew it in the early '80s. The justice of the peace, the late Faustino Acuña, Sr., came to me one evening and handed me some papers to serve on a prominent man, Mr. C. F. Hilton, who had a ranch over in the Sacramento River Valley of the Sacramento Mountains. That locality at the time was in the La Luz precinct and was also in Doña Ana County.

A family by the name of Chatfield was living at La Luz and the complaint against Hilton was sworn to by members of the Chatfield family. The same evening, two of the Chatfield boys came to my house and said that they understood that I had "papers" for Hilton. The papers to be served was a summons to the justice court to answer an attachment made on some rails Hilton had in his possession. The next morning I got an early start for the Sacramento River country and overtook the Chatfield boys a little ways out of La Luz. One of the boys said, "Well, are you going after Hilton?" I told him that I was on my way in line of duty to serve Mr. Hilton with a summons. I knew Mr. Hilton, and knew him to be a fine man in all respects.

The young man replied (for both the boys), "We'll go with you and help you, that old man is going to resist." I told him, "Let Hilton resist; I'll serve the papers, and if he doesn't show up in court, you win the case." "Yes," he said, "but we want to know that these papers are served." I said, "If that is what you want, you can wait at La Luz and find out from my return whether the papers were served."

I went on to the Chatfield ranch on the Sacramento River and I stayed all night with them. They treated me very well. The next morning I saddled my horse. The Chatfield boys saddled their horses too. I saw that they were determined to go with me and I knew that would mean trouble. I surmised that they wanted only a slight excuse to shoot Hilton down. I was determined that they would not have that chance if I could prevent it. One boy was on his horse and the other was standing. I told them that I would get along without them, and if I did need them, I would deputize them in a regular manner.

I went on to the Hilton ranch. There was an old man there. I think he was the cook. I asked him where I could find Mr. Hilton. He told me that Hilton was over on the Bluewater, but was expected home that day. I concluded I would go up after him. I thought that if I found him at Bluewater, I could serve the paper and come back by my brother-in-law's place—Mel Lusk—probably stay all night there and come on home the next day.

However, I met Mr. Hilton about half way over to Bluewater. I served my summons and got in his buggy with him and rode, leading my saddle horse. I stayed all night with him. I studied the situation. I wanted to warn Hilton to be careful of the Chatfields, and yet I didn't want to get mixed up in the feud.

I finally concluded that I would warn him that the Chatfield clan would kill him if they had half a chance.

The next morning I came home by way of Dog Canyon. At that time, the law permitted a constable to collect mileage only when he had to go at least a mile and a half beyond the boundary of his own precinct. This was pretty hard on constables sometimes, when serving in a precinct as large as La Luz precinct was at that time.

When the trial came up before Justice Acuña at La Luz, Mr. Hilton was on hand. I think that he stopped at the D. M. Sutherland home. He and Mr. Sutherland were good friends. When Mr. Hilton learned that I had received nothing for the long trip to serve him with the summons, he pulled out a five dollar bill and handed it to me. I do not remember exactly the result of the trial, although I know that it only seemed to add more fuel to the flames of hate, already in evidence. These same bunch of rails in question at the trial was the cause of the climax to the tragedy. That was the end of my acquaintance with Mr. Hilton. My wife died soon after and I went back to Carlsbad. However, I have been told of many of the circumstances of the final tragedy, which I have always presumed were correct statements. The feud went on.

Hilton had come from Old Mexico in 1884 with a herd of cattle. He settled in the Sacramento River Valley and proceeded to develop a fine ranch in a country then practically unoccupied. He had a partner, an El Paso druggist by the name of Irving. The latter took up a piece of land in what is known as "Irving Flats." A man by the name of James B. Smith, who was a son-in-law of old man Chatfield, jumped the claim.

While Hilton & Irving realized that they could hardly hold the land with Mr. Irving living in El Paso, apparently they did seek to retain possession of some of the improvements on the land and attempted to remove them, including the bunch of rails. As a matter of justice, it seems that they should have been allowed to take the rails away. But this proposition was what the La Luz suit was about. The justice of the peace, on advice of Mr. Sutherland, had made it clear to the Chatfields that there could be no issue as to the title to the lands in justice court, which had no jurisdiction whatever as to land titles. Therefore the issue was strictly over the ownership of the rails.

The climax to the feud came only a short time later, February 14, 1894, according to documents now in evidence. Mr. Hilton with his men had taken wagons up after the rails, to remove them to his place since they were abandoning any contest over the land. The men were in the act of loading the rails when some of the Chatfield men appeared. After dodging between the wagons for a brief time, Smith shot Hilton, killing him instantly.

The body of Hilton was allowed to lay where he fell for many hours, in order that a coroner might be obtained to hold an inquest. It proved impossible to obtain a justice of the peace and an inquest, so the body was taken to the Hilton ranch home, where he was buried the next day. The weather was cold and had been for several months, and considerable difficulty was experienced in getting a grave dug. As it was, only a shallow one was excavated before solid rock was struck.

[Note by the editor of the *Alamogordo News:* The *News* has been supplied with some data on the Hilton murder case supplementary to that given by Mr. Meadows, which are given below.

There were a number of men who remained with the body that day, awaiting the holding of a coroner's jury. Most of these parties were friends of Hilton, but there were also a few Chatfield partisans. One of those there that day has told the editor that it would not have "taken much of a spark to set off the fireworks."

A number of men were armed and the feeling between the two factions was bitter. Thomas Jones, Senior, was Hilton's foreman at the time. He was present that day, and in addition, according to one who was also there, the following men were present where the body lay that day: Thos. Cadenhead, Thomas Jones, Harve Lewis, Joe Logan, Bill Babers, A. O. Chatfield,

Marion Wills, J. D. York, Jas. F. Wayland, Dave Taylor, Will Brownfield, Jud McNair, and a man named McNill.

The body of Mr. Hilton was taken up about a month later and it was found to be frozen and in perfect condition, as if it had been kept in a refrigerator. A brother from Illinois had the body embalmed in El Paso and it was then taken to the former home in Illinois for interment.

Up to his death, Mr. Hilton operated a large ranch and kept a commissary. He had befriended and carried along many a poor ranchman; had supplied them with provisions from time to time. He and Chas. Myers' store at La Luz were the only places over a large region where the ranchmen could obtain provisions. Hilton had a reputation of being fair in all his dealings. His estate was soon closed out and the land went to others. We have the opinion of a reputable citizen now living in Alamogordo that the Hilton murder was really instigated and put over by an El Paso businessman who died a few years ago, and who coveted the Hilton range and water holdings. The Alamogordo man believes that the Chatfields were only pawns in the feud.

Smith was tried in Las Cruces. He was defended by the able and brilliant young attorney, Albert B. Fall. He was acquitted and seemed to have money and influence on tap for his defense. All of the Chatfields, including the son-in-law, Smith, left in a short time. There are men in Alamogordo today who were subpoenaed as character witnesses for Hilton—but they were never called to the witness chair. They do not know why to this day Hilton was painted in black colors, they say, when the opposite was the case].[4]

Chapter 17

✦ ✦ ✦

Making Hay Where No Grass Grows Now

There was quite a little friction between deputies in Pat Garrett's office (sheriff) at Las Cruces in 1897. Jimmie Brent, as fine a man as I ever knew, and R. M. Banner [*sic;* E. E. Banner], Garrett's office deputy, didn't get along at all.

Finally Brent went to Garrett and told him that it was either Banner or himself who would have to leave. Pat told Brent that he hated to lose him, but guessed that Brent would have to go. Jim Brent quit and went to his home in Silver City. This was late in the summer. I stayed with Pat a while longer and never hated to leave anyone as bad as I did him. I did not like Banner very much myself and he tried to make it disagreeable enough for me.

I went to Pat one morning and told him I had bought a mowing machine and rake of Mr. Roualt [*sic;* Rouault] and was going to making hay on the west side of the Organ Mountains. Garrett asked me why not let him in on the hay enterprise? I had bought the machines on credit. Garrett said he would pay for the mower and rake and bear his share of the expenses and we would go it half and half on the profits. I agreed. That was the same year the surveyors were working north out of El Paso for the proposed "White Oaks Ry. line," which eventually turned into the old El Paso & Northeastern, running through Alamogordo.

I went to cutting hay west of the Organs and cut about fifty tons and got it stacked up in fair shape. This was more hay than we could make in the same place at any time in recent years. The hay was sold in Las Cruces and we made a little

Fig. 19a. Aultman, Miller & Co's Buckeye Mower.
Courtesy of New Mexico State University
Library's Archives and Special Collections,
Ms0004, Amador Trade Catalogs, box 2, folder 43,
Aultman, Miller and Co. catalog, c. 1898–1900.

Fig. 19b. "The Buckeye Mower is a Sure Winner," courtesy of New
Mexico State University Library's Archives and Special
Collections, Ms0004, Amador Trade Catalogs, box 2, folder 43,
Aultman, Miller and Co. catalog, c. 1898–1900.

money on it. In passing, it may be stated that this hay land was near where Mr. Garrett eventually met his death.

When I was in the hay camp west of the Organs and about through, my old friend Sixto Garcia, of La Luz, came along and stayed all night with me. He told me of some excellent hay meadows about 15 miles north of El Paso, along the line of the proposed railroad survey. I didn't send Garrett any word, but moved camp over to cut that hay. I found this was as Mr. Garcia told me and as [I] had depended on, for he was a trustworthy man. I established a camp. We had to haul water from the old W. N. Fleck ranch and it took us a day to haul four barrels.[1] No grass grows in that locality now owing to overgrazing and erosion and repeated drouths.

I and my two men got up over 100 tons of hay. Garrett had inquired and found out where I was and phoned down to Steve Mendenhall, of El Paso, who ran a feed store, to have me call him (Garrett) up when I was in El Paso. This was in November. We had had about the last of the hay up when I next went in to El Paso to get some feed for our horses.

I talked to Pat over the phone and he asked me to stay in town until he could get down from Las Cruces. When Pat got down, he remarked in his dry sort of way that I was a pretty tough looking hombre. And I guess I was—I hadn't shaved for a number of weeks. Pat took me over to the old Union Store and bought me a new outfit of clothing, including suit, socks, boots, hat, etc. I was wondering what was the matter with Pat, he was so generous. He told me to go down to Mendenhall's and he would see me in the morning. He gave me ten dollars for expense money.

The next morning we had a long confab sitting on a bale of hay in Mendenhall's place. Pat told me that he wanted me in the office at Las Cruces. I told him I would not go back in the office if R. M. Banner was there. He said: "Well, I guess I will have to let Banner out." I went back to my hay camp and gave the boys instructions how to close up the camp and the next day I rode in to Las Cruces.

I got there about sundown. The next morning I got a shave and put on my new clothes and went down to the office. Banner was still there. He gave me a bunch of papers to be served on parties in the Rincon country, enough work for several days. He was still inclined to make things [as] miserable as possible for me. As I left, I saw Garrett and told him I had enough money [*sic*; duties] to keep me busy for several days. He told me that by the time I got back, he would be rid of Banner.

I was gone about a week and when I got back, Banner was still on the job. I stopped with the Garrett family. I was always made comfortable in the Garrett home and my recollections of my stay in the Garrett home are pleasant memories indeed. When Pat came in I said, "What's the matter with you and Banner; can't you settle up?"

He didn't reply to that question but said, "John, there is another trip for you, a good long one, up to Tularosa." It was a long trip, too, in those days, and you were well aware of the fact if you rode it horseback. I pulled out for Tularosa, leaving Banner in the sheriff's office. I was gone for a week or ten days. When I got back, Fred Lohman was in the sheriff's office, trying to straighten out the books, which had gotten into a mess. I think Fred finally gave it up in disgust and couldn't tell whether Banner owed Garrett or Garrett owed Banner, and Fred was a fine bookkeeper, too.

I worked on for Mr. Garrett for a few months, but I was rapidly nearing the end of my association with him, which had extended off and on for more than 20 years, and which was of a most agreeable nature. Mr. Garrett, as all humans, made his mistakes, but it is not for me to judge nor point them out. He always treated me as a friend and I enjoyed his friendship.[2]

Chapter 18

✦ ⋆ ✦

Calls 'Em Down

John P. Meadows Says Some Plain Things to the
Independent-Democrat Fellow.[1]

Las Cruces, March 10, 1897.

Editor *Doña Ana County Republican:*

Dear Sir: For several months past the disreputable sheet known as the *Independent-Democrat* has in various ways insinuated that James Brent and myself, while out on an official trip, killed two hogs belonging to parties whose names they have thus far failed to reveal. If you will allow me space in your columns I will give full account of our trip at that time, together with the killing of the hogs which appear to be so much worrying the *Democrat.*

About August 1, Sheriff Garrett sent Jim Brent and myself to the mountains to search for the bodies of Colonel Fountain and son. The first night out we stopped with John Bonney at the Gold Camp. The next day we started for the Jarillas, having heard that water was plenty there, and preferring that way rather than to go by Lee's well. Got to north end of White mountains and not finding any water had to ride near summit of Sacramento Mountains to get a drink for ourselves and horses. Camped at Grapevine Springs until evening to let horses rest.

While camped there a man, [a] stranger, came along with whom we had a long talk. This was the only human we met in the mountains. Moved over to the big bluff near Agua Chiquita, short distance from Dog Canyon, and camped that night. Next morning staked horses near bluff, and went in to bluff on foot to make a search. While hunting around in the brush found two musk hogs and killed them. Knocked the tusk out of one of them and brought it to Las Cruces. Showed it to a number of people here.

After making a thorough but fruitless search for the bodies of Colonel Fountain and son, we tried to find a trail from the bluff to Las Cruces, but not succeeding had to come around by J. W. Ward's ranch, where we stopped over night. Left his place next morning after Mr. Ward had kindly given us sufficient bread and coffee to last us on homeward trip. Rode until evening and camped within seven miles of Gold Camp. Arrived at Gold Camp next morning, and still having considerable of the bacon which we had taken with us from Las Cruces, we gave it to John Bonney, as he will vouch. Came home direct from Gold Camp.

This is a correct account of the entire trip which appears to have worried the scrubs on the *Democrat*. Now the *Democrat* claims to have received a letter from "B. & K.," whoever they are, charging that we killed some of their hogs. I have no knowledge as to who "B. & K." may be, and, in fact, I doubt that any such persons exist other than in the elastic imagination of the foul scrubs who do the dirty work on the insignificant rag called a newspaper. If any hogs owned by anyone were killed at that time, Mr. Brent or myself knew nothing of it, and the attempt to connect us therewith shows to what extent some curs will go to injure a man simply because they cannot control him.

I do not believe the *Democrat* ever received any such letter as they claim, but in any event the assertions made therein are a tissue of lies, and the author or authors are contemptible, cowardly liars. I have been a resident of New Mexico for 17 years and all who know me know that I have always conducted myself honorably and attended to my own business. I do not intend to allow anyone to charge me with being a thief and I will not longer submit to the vicious and vituperative spleen which the *Democrat* has thrown at me in the past.

John P. Meadows

Chapter 19

⋆ ⋆ ⋆

Catching a Slippery Cow Thief

While I was deputy sheriff under Pat F. Garrett at Las Cruces in 1898, Kearney, the office deputy for Mr. Garrett, handed me a warrant for a notorious cow thief by the name of Rito Montoya. Montoya's home stamping ground was in the Loma Parda country, not far from Rincon. However, his field of operations extended quite a ways in all directions. I had arrested the fellow before, and he had been in jail several times before and escaped each time in some bold style. The previous time he simply outran the men in the sheriff's office when he got a chance to sprint a little. So when I took the warrant from Kearney's hands I said: "I am going to put that fellow in jail again and if he gets out, you fellows can go after him the next time." I got on my horse and went to Loma Parda by way of Rincon. I stopped with an old Mexican friend all night, by the name of Agipito.

We talked over the first time I had arrested Rito Montoya—we chased Rito through the Caballo Mountains until late in the afternoon. I and my men scattered out to see if we couldn't round him up. In the afternoon late I was on a ridge and saw a man running down the canyon. I guessed that it was Rito, and so it proved to be. When he got down near the river, two of my men were close upon him. The resourceful rascal ran and jumped as far out into the stream as he could. He had his gun in his hand when he jumped. With the other men, I rode up and ordered him to throw his gun out or we would have to shoot him.

He said that his gun was buried in the sand. I told him to dig it out. He found the gun all right—or maybe he had not

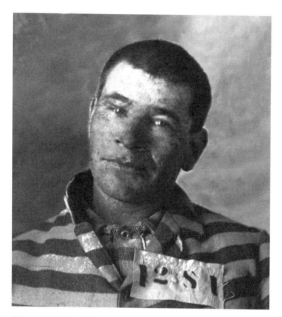

Fig. 20. Rito Montoya, December 1899.
Courtesy of New Mexico State Records
Center and Archives, N.Mex. Dept. of
Corrections, Penitentiary of N.Mex.
photograph collection, inmate
no. 1281.

lost it, which was the more likely. I told him to come out and
surrender and he would be treated all right. He came out and
I arrested him and placed him up behind one of the men and
we rode into Rincon. There I left my horse with A. McClintock,
the pioneer merchant there, and took the train with Rito down
to Las Cruces.

I put him in jail and he stayed only a short time, when as
I told above, he got away by outrunning the officers. He went
over into the Gila country and did not show up in the Loma
Parda country for a long time. Rito was a confirmed thief, similar to what the west has always had, and it was a safe bet that
he would get into trouble with the law again in the course of
time. Rito saw lots of Anglos getting away with the rustling
business and doubtless he thought he could.

One day Garrett said to me: "John, Rito Montoya is back in the Loma Parda country. You had better go up there and see if you can get him." And, as I related, I went up there after him. Agipito, my Mexican friend, told me that he thought probably Rito was down in the Picacho country near Las Cruces. I started back on my horse to Las Cruces to see if I could learn of his whereabouts.

Quite a distance below Rincon on the Jornada Mesa, who should I meet face to face but Rito Montoya, the man I was after. Rito was about half drunk. He had quite an advantage over me had he decided to use it, as I was [on] horseback and he was afoot. My first thought was to pass on by him, jump from my horse and cut down on him. However, he knew me, so I got to talking and eased off my horse. We talked along quite friendly. I asked him for some cigarette papers. I gave him some tobacco to make a cigarette. He surprised me by asking me if I didn't want to take a drink of his wine before I made the cigarette. I said, "Sure!"

He handed me a bottle. I pretended to take a drink and did take a taste and then handed the bottle back to him. When he turned the bottle up to take a drink, I threw my gun on him and told him that I didn't want to kill him, but would do it quick if he didn't drop his gun. I told him that if he didn't keep his hands up until I got hold of his six-shooter, I would kill him.

I put handcuffs on Rito, then we started down the road to Leasburg, where I hoped to catch the next south-bound train for Las Cruces. I was on my horse, herding Rito along as I would a steer, and he was glad enough to walk straight. But I didn't make the train, so had a long wait at Leasburg with Rito under guard all the time. There was an old Mexican at Leasburg who hated Rito so badly he would have liked to kill him. I took Rito in to Las Cruces on the train, leaving my horse at Leasburg until I could recover him. I put Rito in the 'Cruces jail and he stayed there only a few days, when he made quite a spectacular escape.

Rito was allowed to do some work stacking some hay on the back lot of the jail premises. He was on the stack where they could keep track of him. At the side of the stack, Garrett had several of his race horses, munching contentedly at the new mown hay. Soon Rito, who was a splendid horseman, edged to that side of the stack, slid down onto Pat Garrett's favorite horse, and was off like a flash.

Rito rode the horse only to the river, evidently not wanting to keep the horse, as that would give the sheriff too much of an incentive to pursue him. He turned the horse loose and then forded the river and got into the low underbrush and then easily escaped. The race horse was recovered in a short time, in fact was making his own way back.

Rito was never arrested again, so far as I know. The next we heard of him was several years later. He had slipped back into the home country and felt bold enough to attend a dance at Paraje.[1] He and his partner attempted some bad-man stuff and a little constable, who by the way was a sheep-herder by trade, ordered Rito and his partner to hold up their hands. Rito didn't comply and the officer pumped him full of lead, or at least full enough to end his career.

After that, the sheriff at Socorro made the little constable a deputy sheriff. He made a reputation in his shooting of Rito.[2]

Epilogue

Maurice Fulton probably didn't intend to edit John Meadows's stories for publication, although the thirty-eight-page typescript titled "Billy the Kid as I Knew Him" carries the byline "John P. Meadows with Collaboration from Maurice G. Fulton." This exhibits little editing beyond an occasional added word or short phrase. The other forty pages in this manuscript— "Cowboy in Texas," "Overland to California," and several unorganized sections from other stories—show no editing at all.

Fulton may not have believed these reminiscences, but his own sources (when known) were not always impeccable.[1] He had copies of two of the 1931 articles from the *Roswell Daily Record* and perhaps didn't know about the series published in the *Alamogordo News*. His book on the Lincoln County War, edited by Robert N. Mullin, made no obvious use of what Meadows said; for example, Fulton took the Kid straight from his courthouse escape at Lincoln to a friend's home in the Capitan foothills and then to Fort Sumner. Meadows's first-person account, although written some fifty years later, is quite different.

This leads us to the question of what independent sources could confirm or deny of what John Meadows tells us. Did he exaggerate; mix in some big windies; or edit his stories by, for instance, putting himself in situations where he may have had only a peripheral role? How do we judge? His reminiscences are more valuable if there are no serious questions about them.

To continue, using the episode cited just above, Barney Mason left a near-contemporary account of Billy's itinerary following his escape from the courthouse. This would take him to Agua Azul, to John Newcomb's cow camp (Newcomb's ranch or farm was on the Ruidoso), then to Consios [Conejos] Springs and Buffalo Arroyo.[2] Even if the newspaper reported everything accurately, it wouldn't preclude the Kid's presence on the Peñasco, where Billy Mathews's farm adjoined the one being worked by Meadows and Tom Norris. There were rumors and newspaper claims at the time (all untrue) that Billy the Kid *had* sought out and shot Billy Mathews, which lend support to Meadows's report of Billy's visit and his own suspicion that the Kid had come there to kill Mathews. Utley, Nolan, and Fleming seem to agree that Meadows's account (in chapter 3) is creditable.[3]

John Meadows's story about traveling to Pinos Wells, Gran Quivira, the Carrizozo ranch, and then to White Oaks is an episode that begs for confirmation (chapter 1). There are no known independent sources that refer to such a trip in the spring of 1880, but neither is there evidence to discredit it. Between March 10 and May of 1880, Billy's calendar was clear; his whereabouts is not documented anywhere.[4] He may well have been off on a jaunt with his new friend.

This trip would have coincided with the peak of Apache chief Victorio's raiding through southern New Mexico and the army's campaigning against him. This was one of the most violent episodes in New Mexico's history and it might appear now that two cowboys riding off in the face of such a threat is scarcely believable. But close reading of New Mexico newspapers from the early months of 1880 show that this wasn't unusual at all. Isolated sheepherders, miners, mail riders, ranchers, and others died by the dozens, but people didn't stop what they were doing and apparently didn't express much concern about their personal risks.[5] New Mexicans had lived with the threat of Indian raids for hundreds of years.

The civilian casualties from Victorio's assaults were horrific; yet these are scarcely mentioned in the standard histories of that period. The wife of Territorial Governor Lew. Wallace said that in the Apache war ending in October 1880, more than four hundred white persons were scalped and tortured to death. Echoing her, at the beginning of 1881 *The Mesilla News* screamed "Horrible Butcheries. 71 Week's Campaign. 415 Massacres to date." A local resident writing to the secretary of war in June of 1880 claimed that about two hundred people of southern New Mexico had been killed.[6]

Victorio's sweep through western New Mexico in early May of 1880 culminated with his attack on Cooney's Camp, a mining operation on Mineral Creek in the Mogollon Mountains. While histories downgrade the losses there to *three* bodies, *The Grant County Herald* listed *sixty-six* persons killed during the Mogollon raid.[7]

John Meadows's claims of a recent Indian camp at Seven Lakes as well as the sheepherders killed at Pinos Wells are entirely in line with what was happening at the time. We haven't known of such tragedies because the Victorio campaign has always been portrayed as an extended running battle between soldiers and Apaches, with civilians watching on the sidelines. The reality is that the army ignored the severity of non-combatants' losses. This was one of the reasons why the territorial press attacked the military district commander so fiercely.[8]

Another reason why citizen losses are so incompletely known is that undocumented raids extended well into central New Mexico. Early in February, Major Albert Morrow sent one scouting party "northward into the mountains" from Tularosa, New Mexico. They returned after finding only small trails.[9] In April a wagon train bearing freight was captured between Los Lunas and Fort Wingate, while herders were killed at Bear Springs, "which is much farther north than the hostiles have heretofore been." A report from Belen said that seven men were killed in an Indian attack on a railroad camp south of Belen. Two men died west of town and another person had his horse teams taken away; miners were driven out of the Ladron Mountains to seek refuge at Lemitar. A Mexican rancher who saw this raiding party said there were about sixty Indians all told, twenty of them mounted, all with government rifles and belts full of cartridges. The bodies of five men killed close to La Joya were brought in to that village.[10]

Later in the month, Major Curwen McLellan's scouts sought for trails in the Jicarilla Mountains and Sierra Oscura, which are north and west of modern Carrizozo. People in Tularosa thought the Indians were in the vicinity of Rinconada [Canyon] and Carrizosa. By May, the destruction of sheep ranches and murders of herders had shifted west, to Horse Spring and the ranches of the Luna brothers in the Los Lentes valley (now Centerfire Creek) near present-day Luna, New Mexico.[11]

To Billy the Kid at Seven Lakes, it probably did look like Victorio's whole outfit, but the probability is that a branch or splinter party the army never saw, perhaps the sixty raiders seen later west of the Rio Grande, had passed through. The nature and timing of what Meadows and Billy witnessed are consistent with what we know from contemporary newspaper accounts and add plausibility to the story about their trip to Pinos Wells and Gran Quivira.

A third example concerns Meadows's account of where the Kid went between the time he rode out of Camp Grant (not Thomas) in Arizona and when he appeared some time later on the Pecos. Historians and indeed newspaper accounts from 1877 have written of a fairly rapid journey via Knight's ranch south of Silver City and the Mesilla Valley, perhaps in company for part of the way with a gang of outlaws headed by Jessie Evans, and then on to Seven Rivers in the Pecos River Valley.[12]

An alternative reconstruction of this interval notes that 7 1/2 weeks elapsed between when the Kid killed Frank Cahill at Camp Grant on August 17, 1877, and when the murderer, still known as Henry Antrim, was spotted with some horse thieves at Cookes Canyon on October 9. Years ago, the late William Keleher claimed that Billy had spent several weeks in and about Georgetown, New Mexico, citing a Sigmund Lindauer as his source, and Donald Cline seemed to agree although he gave no authority. Jerry Weddle had the Kid pausing for a couple of weeks at Knight's ranch and then for an indefinite period in September at places in the Mimbres River Valley, including a ranch northeast of Georgetown. His references included reminiscences by Anthony Conner and Chauncey Truesdell, and several interviews.[13]

Enough research has been done to make these two reconstructions, which are actually complementary, almost beyond challenge. The early history of the Kid's career given in the first seven chapters of Pat Garrett's *The Authentic Life of Billy, the Kid* has long since been discredited as the wild imaginings of Garrett's ghost writer, Ash Upson. But a comparison of these chapters with Meadows's reminiscences in the first six paragraphs of chapter 2 in this book reveals that these are basically the same story, even to the veiled reference to John Kinney's ranch on the Rio Grande.[14] The version in Garrett's book is greatly elaborated and the one by Meadows is much simpler, but both are built around the Kid's alleged odyssey in Old Mexico with a Mexican partner. Meadows's version includes a few details that can be checked out, such as the existence of Lapoint's Saloon in Las Cruces, New Mexico.

Lawrence Lapoint edited a Las Cruces newspaper, the *Eco del Rio Grande,* between July 1875 and March of 1878. Unfortunately only a few numbers have survived. Lapoint had another principal business in that he served as register of the La Mesilla Land Office in 1875. A Mesilla paper reported that he moved his family and the *Eco* office into a new building in Las Cruces about the second week of September in 1877. We can also show that a decade before, back in 1866 and 1868, Lapoint had held retail liquor licenses in Doña Ana County, and beginning on December 8, 1879, he again paid for one. Although none of the newspapers in Las Cruces and Mesilla advertised a saloon or other business with his name attached, the Las Cruces *Thirty-Four* did carry several two-line ads in 1880 for "Wines and liquors of all kinds" and "the best whiskey" at Lapoint's. The following year a display ad appeared for him as a retail merchant, which included liquor and tobacco, in the *Rio Grande Republican.*[15]

It is not impossible that Lapoint had a saloon as well as a newspaper office in 1877 and that the Kid could have dealt monte there before going on to the Pecos, as John Meadows relates. More than likely though, if this happened at all it was after 1878, because Lapoint was not one of the twenty-eight retail liquor dealers in Doña Ana County who paid a tax to the territory between May 1, 1877, and May 1, 1878.[16] Donald Cline believed that Billy did spend some time in the Mesilla Valley and possibly rode with John Kinney's bunch of rustlers and horse thieves, while other historians are silent about this interval in the Kid's life.[17] Once again, the conclusion is that what Meadows said is plausible, if not proven.

The intended point of this third example is that there is no need to assert that part of Garrett's biography of Billy the Kid was based upon Ash Upson's imagination. It is more likely that the early chapters in Garrett's book and John Meadows's parallel account as well originated with the Kid himself; that this was the past he concocted for himself. Meadows nowhere referred to Garrett's biography, and his own version is sufficiently different to show that it was not based upon reading the book. As Fulton suspected long ago, the actual explanation may be that Billy himself laid a false trail to conceal his own recent past as well as to protect his friends.[18] Consistency was not necessary if the intention was to mislead or to at least sow confusion. Only in recent years has it been possible to unravel some of these fantasies. As his notoriety grew, so too did the young outlaw's talent for manipulating the press. The most outrageous fabrication—of his castle on the plains of eastern New Mexico—was datelined from Fort Sumner, New Mexico, just four days prior to his death on July 14, 1881.[19] Whether he made up this particular fable or not, the Kid would probably have been amused by some of the creative accounts of his own death.[20]

John Meadows was unusually careful to qualify the stories of Billy's escapades by saying that a great deal of his information was from the mouth of the Kid himself, as it may well have been. Whether it was true or not is another question, and the claim that he himself may have shot Robert Beckwith is demonstrably not so.[21] The version of Billy's earlier life recounted by Meadows was plausible at the time because the Kid himself was said to be the source.

Meadows distinguished what he had seen or experienced personally from what he was told, and at one time expressed his concern for correctness in this way:

> My understanding is I might be making a mistake and
> if I do, I will thank any old timer to put me straight. I
> want the truth to go here tonight. I don't want to say

nothing to offend anybody. I am going to tell the truth and let the chips fall where they may. If I make a mistake, I want somebody to put me straight.[22]

By the 1930s, Meadows's accounts were what he believed. He had probably told and retold them hundreds of times and polished them to where they were entertaining as well as believable. His style made these reminiscences interesting and in large part they had the ring of truth. He was never boring and did not repeat himself when telling a story. The integrity they retained for so many years, without reference to written notes or apparently to published books and articles, is remarkable. With respect to the details, in most instances we are left with Agnes Morley Cleaveland's comment on her own work, that "it could have happened that way."

John Meadows was also careful to place events in time. Apart from three episodes that he dated to 1881 while independent sources place them in 1882, and one in 1886 for which he gave an 1887 date, he appears to have had a reliable memory for time. Usually but not always he remembered personal names correctly. He may have injected himself into situations where in reality he had a less prominent role or even none at all; this is suggested by his version of how Billy Wilson was granted a pardon. Philip Rasch's research has shown that John Meadows was not involved with this pardon effort.[23]

We noted earlier that Meadows did not always tell everything he knew or should have known about some episodes, and anyone who uses his reminiscences to document these happenings should bear this in mind. This kind of lapse was not a failure or deception on his part, but rather an awareness that he recounted these reminiscences as stories, not as a witness in a courtroom. He was free to include or leave out any details he chose, and on occasion he seems to have done just that.

In addition to the cited instances where details, names, and dates in Meadows's reminiscences were compared against contemporary sources, confirmations have been sought for other incidents and names. Without getting overly analytical, the two most serious discrepancies were noted in chapters 4 and 9. A contemporary source showed that it was a young hired man, not the rancher's two sons, who was murdered at J. J. Jackson's ranch near Point of Sands. Again, Rito Montoya's final capture, imprisonment, and gruesome death were entirely different from what Meadows said. In both cases he relied entirely on secondhand information from unknown sources and he probably introduced elements from other stories without realizing it. The present writer is only too aware of how easily this can happen.

This man who knew Billy the Kid should be forgiven for errors or overstatements because the temptation for someone on the periphery of historic events to enhance their own role can be almost irresistible.[24] One way in which John Meadows showed restraint was that none of his stories involved the power figures of his day. These would be people like Thomas Catron, W. L. Rynerson, W. W. Cox, Oliver Lee, A. B. Fall, Colonel Albert Jennings Fountain, Joseph C. Lea, Charles B. Eddy, and W. J. McDonald. His contacts with some of these persons can be documented, although later in time.[25] Perhaps the explanation is that they were not part of his personal world and he wisely refrained from making it appear that they had been.

There is no intention to be unduly critical. The old deputy was a fine storyteller and he had a wide range of experiences to draw upon. By the 1930s it would have become apparent that his listeners most wanted to hear about Billy the Kid. These tales were also the ones that can most easily be checked against other sources, and when this is done, John Meadows fares well. His accounts have been cited especially by Utley, but also by Sonnichsen, Metz, Rasch, Nolan, and Wilson.[26]

Where he alone is the source, one can enjoy and accept his reminiscences. These end more than thirty years before his own death. Jack Potter and Dee Harkey brought their stories down to about the same point in time, though both lived a good fifty years later. All of them recognized that what their listeners or readers wanted to know about was a New Mexico that no longer existed: one without railroads, paved roads, and electricity, not to mention indoor plumbing and automobiles!

Fig. 21. Angus VV Ranch chuck wagon and round-up camp on the Rio Ruidoso, N.Mex., 1896. Photo by C. W. Marks. Courtesy of the Museum of New Mexico, neg. no. 89,752.

The days of a Wild West were beyond their own memories, but not so long ago that a few old-timers who were still around could not recall them.

The end of the nineteenth century also marked the closing of an era, and a contemporary writer in a neighboring state aptly labeled one of his books *History That Will Never Be Repeated.*[27] Within a few years the old ways would seem exotic, foreign, almost foreign, and for an audience in the twentieth century the sensation must have been much like what Billy the Kid felt on his first train ride from Las Vegas to Santa Fe, New Mexico, twenty years earlier. The Kid failed to recognize that his time was over and the days of unbridled lawlessness were ending, unlike many of his peers who took Pat Garrett's advice and left the country. By not seeing this, it cost him his life.

Now in 1900 another era was closing, and those who had been part of it had to find new roles. For the army generals who began their careers fighting Indians, it took a shock like the 1915 Battle of Agua Prieta, opposite Douglas, Arizona, to make them realize that the army they knew had become obsolescent.[28] For the veterans of western settlement, it was the innovations mentioned above that transformed them into old-timers, who now told others how it used to be.

The Old West became the stuff of dime novels and motion pictures. Writers now looked for "local color," "source material," and picturesque characters. Billy the Kid might have loved this, but he was too tied to the old ways as he told John Meadows, as well as on the wrong side of the law. It was Meadows's law-abiding contemporaries who helped to create the image of the Old West as a land of cowboys, Indians, robbers, and six-guns. In so doing they confirmed that the era had indeed passed into history, leaving a rich heritage as a resource for entertainment and the literary pursuits of novelists and historians.

Notes

Introduction

1. Mrs. Jo Anderson, personal communication, Alamogordo, N.Mex., May 28, 1996; Web Page for the 5th Georgia Infantry Regiment CSA at http://www.researchonline.net/gacw/unit21.htm; see also chapter 4.

2. "Cowboy in Texas," pp. 1–14 of manuscript "Billy the Kid as I Knew Him," by John P. Meadows, in Philip J. Rasch files, Lincoln State Monument, Lincoln, N.Mex.; *Alamogordo News,* Oct. 17, 24, 31; Nov. 14, 21, 28, 1935.

3. Meadows, "Cowboy in Texas," in Rasch files; *Alamogordo News,* Sept. 12, 26; Dec. 1, 12, 19, 1935; Jan. 9, 1936.

4. *Roswell Daily Record,* Feb. 17, 1931, p. 8.

5. *Roswell Daily Record,* Feb. 20, 1931, p. 3; Feb. 26, p. 1; Feb. 27, pp. 1, 4.

6. *Roswell Daily Record,* Feb. 27, 1931, pp. 1, 4.

7. Frazier Hunt, *The Tragic Days of Billy the Kid* (New York: Hastings House, 1956), 201–4, 214, 300–302.

8. T. Dudley Cramer, *The Pecos Ranchers in the Lincoln County War* (Orinda, Calif.: Branding Iron Press, 1996), 171–74. Jim Bradshaw, Archivist, personal communication, J. Evetts Haley History Center, Midland, Texas, Feb. 4, 2002.

9. *Alamogordo News,* July [sic; June] 25, 1936, pp. 1, 2.

10. Marriages, Book 1, p. 37, at Otero County Clerk's office, Alamogordo, N.Mex.; National Archives and Records Administration (NA), 12th Census (1900), Population Schedules, Precinct #3, Otero County, N.Mex., Microfilm Publication T623 Roll 1001. *Alamogordo Advertiser,* June 25, 1936, p. 1.

11. *Rio Grande Republican,* March 10, 1883, p. 3; NA, 10th Census (1880), Population Schedules, Precinct #5, Lincoln County, and Enumeration District #37, San Miguel County, N.Mex., Microfilm Publication T9 Rolls 802 and 803; New Mexico State

Records Center and Archives (NMSRCA), Territorial Archives of New Mexico, Reel 41.

12. *The Golden Era* (Lincoln, N.Mex.), Aug. 6, Nov. 5, 1885, both p. 1.

13. Mrs. Jo Anderson, personal communication; Lincoln County Transcripts, vol. A, Misc. Contracts and Agreements, p. 47, at Otero County Clerk's office, Alamogordo, N.Mex.

14. C. L. Sonnichsen, *Tularosa: Last of the Frontier West* (Albuquerque: University of New Mexico Press, 1980, 2nd ed.), 125, 310. *Rio Grande Republican,* April 15, 1898, p. 2.

15. Leon C. Metz, *Pat Garrett: The Story of a Western Lawman* (Norman: University of Oklahoma Press, 1974), 149–59. *Independent Democrat,* March 25, 1896, p. 3; *Doña Ana County Republican,* March 11, 1897, p. 1;

16. *Doña Ana County Republican,* April 1, 1897, p. 1; *Independent Democrat,* March 30, 1898, p. 2; *Rio Grande Republican,* April 8, 1898, p. 3, April 22, 1898, p. 3, May 20, 1898, p. 3, July 8, 1898, p. 3, December 23, 1898, p. 3.

17. Metz, *Pat Garrett,* 161–62; *Rio Grande Republican,* April 8, 1898, p. 3.

18. Metz, *Pat Garrett,* 164–71; Sonnichsen, *Tularosa,* 159–64; A. M. Gibson, *The Life and Death of Colonel Albert Jennings Fountain* (Norman: University of Oklahoma Press, 1965), 266–68; *Rio Grande Republican,* July 8, 1898, p. 3.

19. *Rio Grande Republican,* June 2, 1899, p. 1, June 9, 1899, pp. 1–2, June 16, 1899, pp. 1–2; Gibson, *Life and Death,* 271–81; Sonnichsen, *Tularosa,* 174–90; William A. Keleher, *The Fabulous Frontier* (Albuquerque: University of New Mexico Press, 1962, rev. ed.), 257–76.

The individual John Meadows referred to as John Lawrence was probably the same person as the John Laran he named in chapter 12. Don Hampton Biggers called him John Larn and said his killing was an event of more than passing interest in the Fort Griffin country. Larn served a single term as sheriff of Shackelford County, Texas, and owned a fine ranch near Fort Griffin, but then began a wholesale accumulation of other people's cattle. His neighbors tired of this, and upon entering his cowpen one morning Larn found himself covered by numerous armed men. He surrendered, was taken to the county seat at Albany and chained in the little wooden jail. A mob entered the place that night, riddled Larn's body with bullets, and then silently stole away. Biggers thought this happened in 1877; see *Buffalo Guns & Barbed Wire: Two Frontier Accounts: A Combined Reissue of Pictures of the Past and History That Will Never Be Repeated,* by Don Hampton Biggers (Lubbock: Texas Tech University Press, 1991), 80–81.

Selman had a checkered career but lived on as a relic of another age until shot down by a federal marshal; see Metz, *Pat Garrett,* 201; also the same author's *John Selman, Gunfighter* (Norman: University of Oklahoma Press, 1980, 2nd ed.).

20. *Rio Grande Republican,* December 23, 1898, p. 3.

21. *Rio Grande Republican,* April 12, 1899, p. 3.

22. NA, 12th Census (1900), Population Schedules, Precinct #3, Otero County, N.Mex., T623 Roll 1001; NMSRCA, Archdiocese of Santa Fe, Santa Rita Parish, Carrizozo, N.Mex., Marriages 1869–1956, "Registro de los Casamientos del Condado de Lincoln, desde 1869–1903" (microfilm), p. 10.

23. Philip J. Rasch, "The Horrell War," *New Mexico Historical Review* 31(3): 228 (1956); John P. Wilson, *Merchants, Guns, and Money: The Story of Lincoln County and Its Wars* (Santa Fe: Museum of New Mexico Press, 1987), 44.

24. Mrs. Lucille Marr, personal communication, Tularosa, N.Mex., June 18, 1996; New Mexico Bureau of Vital Records, August 7, 1996; St. Francis de Paula Parish registry office, May 15, 2001; Marriages, Book 1, p. 37, at Otero County Clerk's office; NA, 12th Census (1900), Population Schedules, Precinct #3, Otero County, N.Mex., T623 Roll 1001.

25. Miscellaneous, Book 97, p. 130, at Otero County Clerk's office; NA, 13th Census (1910), Population Schedules, Precinct #2, Otero County, N.Mex., T624 Roll 916.

26. *Alamogordo News,* June 28, 1900, p. 4; *The Tularosa Democrat,* Jan. 7, Feb. 25, 1904, both p. 4; *Otero County Advertiser,* June 15, 1907, p. 4.

27. Sonnichsen, *Tularosa,* 90; Carole Larson, *Forgotten Frontier: The Story of Southeastern New Mexico* (Albuquerque: University of New Mexico Press, 1993), 231.

28. Deed Records, Book 11, pp. 295–96, Book 13, pp.

221–22, Book 17, p. 174, Book 47, pp. 18–19, Book 49, p. 332, Book 78, p. 451, Book 81, p. 359; Miscellaneous, Book 40, p. 550; Quit Claim Deeds, Book 79, p. 85; Release Records, Book 81, p. 377, all at Otero County Clerk's office; *Tularosa Valley Tribune,* April 18, 1914, p. 8; Oct. 7, 1916, p. 1.

29. Mrs. Lucille Marr, personal communication, Tularosa, N.Mex., June 18 and July 2, 1996. NA, 14th Census (1920), Population Schedules, Precinct #3, Otero County, N.Mex., T625 Roll 1077.

30. Liquor, Occupation & Gambling Licenses, 1899–1979, pp. 46–49 at Otero County Clerk's office.

31. *Tularosa Valley Tribune,* April 22, 1916, p. 8, Oct. 7, 1916, p. 1.

32. *Alamogordo News,* Feb. 16, 1933, p. 6; Keleher, *Fabulous Frontier,* 267; Gibson, *Life and Death,* 214–15, 249.

33. Minute Book (#2), Village of Tularosa, April 6, 1926, to Dec. 2, 1936, pp. 4, 10–20, 23, 42–43, 67, 75.

34. *Alamogordo News,* Feb. 2, 16, 1933, both p. 6; *Alamogordo Advertiser,* Feb. 2, 1933, p. 1; Will Book 1, p. 196; Probate File #533; Deed Records, Book 102, pp. 33–34; Mortgage Deeds, Book 100, pp. 83–85; all at Otero County Clerk's office.

35. Deed Records, Book 102, pp. 189–90, at Otero County Clerk's office.

36. Charles F. Coan, *A History of New Mexico, vol. 3* (Chicago and New York: The American Historical Society Inc., 1925), 450–51; *Alamogordo Advertiser,* June 25, 1936, p. 1; *Alamogordo News,* June 25, 1936, p. 1.

37. Tax Deeds, Book 113, p. 168, at Otero County Clerk's office.

38. *Alamogordo News,* Sept. 5, 1935, p. 3; Jan. 23, 30; Feb. 6, 1936, all p. 1; Gibson, *Life and Death,* 249, 260.

39. See note 2 above, also "Overland to California," pp. 15–28, and "Billy the Kid As I Knew Him," pp. 29–66, by John P. Meadows, all in Philip J. Rasch files, Lincoln State Monument, Lincoln, N.Mex. Although Meadows's reminiscences of Billy the Kid comprise about thirty-eight pages or almost half of the transcript, this last-cited title is used as the bibliographic reference for this manuscript.

40. Jean M. Burroughs, *On the Trail: The Life and Tales of "Lead Steer" Potter* (Santa Fe: Museum of New Mexico Press, 1980).

41. Ibid., 51.

42. *Roswell Daily Record,* March 4, 1931, p. 6.

43. Dee Harkey, *Mean as Hell* (Albuquerque: University of New Mexico Press, 1948).

44. Mrs. Christine Myers, personal communication, July 29, 2003.

45. Agnes Morley Cleaveland, *No Life for a Lady* (Boston: Houghton Mifflin Co., 1941), 276.

46. Ibid., 166.

47. Loraine Lavender, personal communication, c. 1983–1986.

48. Larson, *Forgotten Frontier;* Sonnichsen, *Tularosa.*

49. Wilson, *Merchants, Guns, and Money,* 131.

50. Larson, *Forgotten Frontier,* 27, 67–71, 281; Robert K. Hill Jr., "Settlement of the Southern Sacramentos, 1880 to 1912; Weed, Avis, Pinon, and Environs," *The Greater Llano Estacado Southwest Heritage* 13(2): 14–22; Robert Kermit Smith, Jr., "Sacramento Mountain Pioneers," *The Greater Llano Estacado Southwest Heritage* 14(1): 1–4, 18–20.

51. Keleher, *Fabulous Frontier;* Larson, *Forgotten Frontier;* Elvis E. Fleming, *Captain Joseph C. Lea: From Confederate Guerrilla to New Mexico Patriarch* (Las Cruces, N.Mex.: Yucca Tree Press, 2002).

Chapter 1

1. Meadows and his companion Tom Norris left west Texas for New Mexico between February 1 and 10, 1880, by way of Quitaque and Tulia, Texas, then to Puerto de Luna on the Pecos River in eastern New Mexico. They rode into Fort Sumner, N.Mex. in March according to Meadows, and on August 17, 1880, he left Seven Rivers with Norris and Tom Johnson heading west toward California (*Alamogordo News,* Sept. 26, Oct. 3, Oct. 10, 1935, all p. 1). This first meeting must have been in early March, and the other events described in the first chapter would have taken place in the spring of 1880.

2. The name persists today. Stinking Springs is about fifteen miles east of the present community of Fort Sumner. On December 23, 1880, Sheriff Pat Garrett and his posse trapped the Kid and his gang there, killing Charlie Bowdre and capturing the rest.

The timing, if not the arithmetic, suggests that these cows included the twenty-two head of Chisum cattle the Kid made off with on March 10, 1880 (see Robert M. Utley, *Billy the Kid: A Short and Violent Life* [Lincoln: University of Nebraska Press, 1989], 133). Perhaps Billy had liberated stock from other owners as well, although the version of Meadows's story in the April 16, 1936, *Alamogordo News* claimed that the Kid had acquired these cattle by dealing monte with Pete Maxwell's sheep herders and sheep shearers. Quién sabe?

3. Plaza Larga Creek is in present-day Quay County, south of Tucumcari, N.Mex. The 1880 Census population schedule does not show a Pankey there. National Archives (NA), 10th Census (1880), Population Schedules, Precinct #22 ("Hamlet of Cañon Largo"), San Miguel County, N.Mex., Microfilm Publication T9 Roll 803.

4. The 1880 census, taken June 15 at Fort Sumner, listed H. A. ("Beaver"?) Smith as a grocer, living in a dwelling that obviously lay close by the Maxwell house. NA, 10th Census (1880), Enumeration District #37 ("Sunnyside and Fort Sumner"), San Miguel County, N.Mex., T9 Roll 803.

5. The same schedule listed John Holand, age seventy-one, as a carpenter and also postmaster.

6. The 1880 Fort Sumner population schedule shows no one by this name living there, nor was there any indication of a restaurant.

7. Pinos Wells was a small community near Cedarvale in present Torrance County, N.Mex. A prominent New Mexico political leader, Colonel J. Francisco Chávez, owned a ranch at Pinos Wells and was assassinated there on the evening of November 26, 1904 (see Tibo Chávez, "Colonel José Francisco Chávez, 1833–1904," *Rio Grande History* no. 8 (1978): 6–9.

Sunnyside, referred to twice above, at that time was a settlement a half-dozen miles north along the Pecos from old Fort Sumner. In 1910 the post office name of Sunnyside was changed to Fort Sumner.

8. No map location found. My estimate is that Seven Lakes lies in the south-central part of Township 1 North Range 19 East, to either side of US 285 in the northeastern corner of Lincoln County. At least six ephemeral lakes are shown there on the U.S. Geological Survey's Loco Draw 7.5-minute quadrangle map.

9. Nobody has chronicled all of the depredations by Victorio and other splinter groups of Apaches. These were at a peak in March and April of 1880; see Dan L. Thrapp, *Victorio and the Mimbres Apaches* (Norman: University of Oklahoma Press, 1974), 266–74; and Joseph A. Stout, Jr., *Apache Lightning: The Last Great Battles of the Ojo Calientes* (New York: Oxford University Press, 1974), 128–36. Most of the raids were in southern New Mexico. However, Billy might have been right about a group of Victorio's Indians being responsible for the deaths he saw; see the epilogue for a more detailed discussion.

10. One scientific devil was Adolph Bandelier, who visited Gran Quivira in January 1883 and found a considerable amount of woodwork remaining in the larger of the two churches but did not mention a cross (Adolph F. Bandelier, *Final Report of Investigations among the Indians of the Southwestern United States, Carried on Mainly in the Years from 1880 to 1885*, part 2 [Cambridge, Mass.: John Wilson and Son, 1892], 286). Lieutenant Charles C. Morrison's field party surveyed the ruins in the summer of 1877 and described the church as even more intact, but did not note a cross (Charles C. Morrison, "Executive and Descriptive Report . . . Field Season of 1877," Appendix F to Appendix NN of *Annual Report of the Chief of Engineers for 1878* (Serial Set #1846), 1558.

11. Red Lake lies at the head of Ancho Gulch, about fourteen miles north of Carrizozo, N.Mex.

12. Carrizozo Spring is about 1.5 miles north of Carrizozo, N.Mex.

13. No such letter is known to have survived, but the substance of this arrangement is confirmed in Wallace's 1908 newspaper interview; see Frederick Nolan, *The West of Billy the Kid* (Norman: University of Oklahoma Press, 1998), 195–96.

14. In the spring of 1880 "Sligh" [J. E. Sligh], who became an early editor-publisher of the White Oaks *Golden Era,* described

the new community as follows: "The town has about five hundred inhabitants, two restaurants, four saloons, three stores, blacksmith and carpenter shops, etc., and a variety show in embryo, Mitchell and troop from Santa Fe are here" (*Supplement to Thirty-four*, May 5, 1880, p. 1). White Oaks was platted in May 1880.

15. "Billy the Kid as I Knew Him," pp. 29–66, by John P. Meadows, in Philip J. Rasch files, Lincoln State Monument, Lincoln, N.Mex.; *Alamogordo News*, April 16 and May 7, 14, 1936, all p. 1.

Chapter 2

1. In 1877 Lawrence Lapoint was editor-publisher of the *Eco del Rio Grande* newspaper at Las Cruces. Whether he had another business at this time is not known for sure. See the epilogue for more discussion.

2. This incident took place on August 29, 1879, and as Meadows says, it was a sequel to the Lincoln County War. For other versions of what happened see Frederick Nolan, *The Lincoln County War: A Documentary History* (Norman: University of Oklahoma Press, 1992), 394–395.

3. "Billy the Kid as I Knew Him," by John P. Meadows, in Philip J. Rasch files, Lincoln State Monument, Lincoln, N.Mex.; *Roswell Daily Record*, March 2 and 3, 1931, both p. 6.

Chapter 3

1. A remote area in the northeastern corner of present Chaves County, N.Mex., about twenty miles east of the Pecos River.

2. Meadows greatly understated the impact of the raid on White Oaks by Billy the Kid and his gang of cutthroats, as the citizens termed them, the evening of November 20, 1880. The outlaws carried off horses, provisions, rifles and other plunder. Although the people appealed to Fort Stanton for help, the post adjutant denied their request, citing the *Posse Comitatus* Act. See NA, Microfilm Publication M-1097, Roll 6, Register of Letters Received by Headquarters, District of New Mexico, 1880–1881, vol. 14 #3882; also Frederick Nolan, *The West of Billy the Kid* (Norman: University of Oklahoma Press, 1998), 233; and Michael

F. Knight, NA, to John P. Wilson, 7 October 2002 (citing a Nov. 25, 1880 response to Postmaster at White Oaks, in Letters Sent, Fort Stanton).

3. Meadows disremembered Carlyle's first name, which was James, and the date, which was November 27, 1880. Most sources call the site of this gunfight the Greathouse ranch; Red Cloud was also the name of an early mine and mining camp in the Gallinas Mountains prospect region.

Note that the Kid didn't deny shooting Jim Carlyle when he talked with Meadows. Dave Rudabaugh and Billy Wilson were also present, and when Wilson denied two months later that he had shot Carlyle, Rudabaugh retorted that "You are a damned liar. We all three shot at him. You and I fired one shot apiece and Kid twice" (*Las Vegas Daily Optic*, January 21, 1881, p. 1).

4. As Utley explains in *Billy the Kid: A Short and Violent Life* (Lincoln: University of Nebraska Press, 1989), p. 264, it must have been Godfrey Gauss, not Nunnelly, who shouted to Olinger.

5. Utley in *Billy the Kid*, 179–81, 186–87, 202–3, 261–63 cited this conversation between Meadows and the Kid a number of times. Utley concluded, as did I, that Meadows probably knew the Kid well and that his recollections largely ring true.

6. "Billy the Kid as I Knew Him," by John P. Meadows, in Philip J. Rasch files, Lincoln State Monument, Lincoln, N.Mex.; *Roswell Daily Record,* March 3, 1931, p. 6; *Alamogordo News,* May 14 and 21, 1936, both p. 1; June 11, p. 5, and June 25, 1936, p. 2.

As explained before, Meadows exaggerated the length of time he acted as a deputy. Garrett served as Doña Ana County sheriff for about 4 1/2 years, 1896–1900. Meadows was living in Tularosa by 1899.

Chapter 4

1. *Alamogordo News,* Feb. 6, 1936, p. 1.

2. J. J. Maxwell reported in 1879 that he had found good water near Whitewater and asked to be appointed U.S. Forage Agent there. Whitewater Spring, "situated in the white sands near the Point of Sands well," fell out of use before 1915.

The Las Cruces *Thirty-Four* carried a report of this murder. According to the paper, four Mexicans drove off all (9) of Maxwell's horses on September 23, 1880. Six broke away and Maxwell was able to track the thieves, three of whom doubled back for the escaped horses. At the ranch once again, they murdered a young man named George McIntyre, a recent arrival from Iowa, whom Maxwell had left at the ranch. The newspaper did not mention any sons. Meadows evidently confused elements from two separate incidents, something that may have happened with his explanation of Rito Montoya's demise as well (chapter 19). See NA, M-1072 Roll 6, Letters Sent 1880, vol. 20, p. 297; M-1097 Roll 6, Register of Letters Received 1879–1880, vol. 13, pp. 107, 138; O. E. Meinzer and R. F. Hare, *Geology and Water Resources of Tularosa Basin, New Mexico,* USGS Water Supply Paper 343 (Washington, D.C.: Government Printing Office, 1915), 265; *Thirty-Four,* Sept. 29, 1880, p. 2.

3. This incident was not reported in the surviving issues of *The Mesilla News* or the Las Cruces *Thirty-Four,* nor does it appear to have been mentioned in military records. The high level of violence and civilian deaths in the late summer of 1880 have been ignored by historians, and many incidents have gone unnoticed.

4. A wagon train with eleven Mexican teamsters was destroyed here on October 13, 1879. The same day, the Apaches killed six New Mexico volunteers in an ambush that apparently became a running fight; see Dan L. Thrapp, *Victorio and the Mimbres Apaches* (Norman: University of Oklahoma Press, 1974), 246, and Las Cruces *Thirty-Four* for Oct. 15 and 22, 1879.

5. He may well have been cutting forage for Fort Cummings. On September 4, 1880, Colonel George Buell at Fort Cummings was sent authorization for his quartermaster to purchase one or two hundred thousand pounds of forage (i.e., grass or hay) at a price not to exceed 5 1/2 cents per pound (NA, M-1072 Roll 6, Letters Sent 1880, vol. 20, p. 303).

6. Neither this incident nor the one that Meadows placed a day or so later at Apache Tejo were mentioned in *The Mesilla News, The Grant County Herald, Thirty-Four,* or in military

correspondence of the period. The September 1880 monthly post return for Fort Cummings unfortunately is missing, and the Letters Sent and Letters Received files for that post begin only in late October. The three newspapers do chronicle a swirl of violence around Fort Cummings between September 5 and 9, 1880, including one stagecoach taken fifteen or sixteen miles east of the fort and a firefight that left one soldier dead and three wounded (*The Grant County Herald,* Sept. 11, p. 2, Sept. 18, 1880, p. 3; *The Mesilla News,* Sept. 18, 1880, p. 2; *Thirty-Four,* Sept. 8, p. 2, Sept. 15, 1880, p. 3). As Thrapp (*Victorio,* p. 207) notes, such incidents were part of an endless series. The incidents that Meadows tells us about may well have happened as he described them.

7. Most of the Letters Sent from Fort Webster from January–August 1852, when it was at its original location at the Santa Rita Copper Mines a few miles north of Apache Tejo, survive in National Archives Microfilm Publication M-1102 Roll 5. These letters indicate that relations with the Apaches were generally peaceful, if tense. Boundary Commissioner John R. Bartlett gave refuge to two Mexican boys from Sonora, who escaped from the Apaches, while at the Copper Mines in late June 1852. And he took possession of the girl Inez Gonzales there. Apache Tejo was not mentioned at the time. The Army did sign a contract with John Fitzgerald in April to establish a farm to furnish Fort Webster with forage and vegetables, but this was to be on the Mimbres River (Jerry D. Thompson, editor, "With the Third Infantry in New Mexico, 1851–1853; The Lost Diary of Private Sylvester W. Matson," *The Journal of Arizona History* 31(4) (1990): 369, 399. As for "Apache Bill," nothing is known beyond what Meadows says. So once more we have a "could have happened this way" situation; plausible but unconfirmed. As for what Meadows says about Apache Tejo at the time of his visit, a person named Charles Davis had requested appointment as forage agent there on July 28, 1880; see NA, M-1097 Roll 6, Register of Letters Received, 1879–1881, vol. 14, p. 418.

8. "Overland to California," pp. 15–28 of manuscript "Billy the Kid as I Knew Him" by Meadows, in Rasch files; also *Alamogordo News,* October 3 and 10, 1935, both p. 1; Feb. 6, 1936, p. 1. Keleher in his *The Fabulous Frontier; Twelve New Mexico Items*

(Albuquerque: University of New Mexico Press, 1962, rev. ed.), pp. 299–321, included a biography of William Ashton Hawkins.

Chapter 5

1. Actually Virden, N.Mex. Duncan is a few miles downstream, in Arizona.

2. In New Mexican Spanish, Colorado sounds like Colorow. But the only Colorado in southern New Mexico was the settlement now called Rodey, just south of Hatch, N.Mex. There was a sutler's store at Fort Cummings, the ruins of which are still standing; it lay immediately south of the original Fort Cummings enclosure. The railroad siding of Florida is about seven miles southeast of Cookes Spring but it did not exist until the Santa Fe Railway built its line from Hatch to Deming in 1881. What Meadows meant is uncertain.

3. *Alamogordo News,* Oct. 10, 1935, p. 1; "Overland to California," by John P. Meadows, in Philip J. Rasch files, Lincoln State Monument, Lincoln, N.Mex. Pat Coghlan, "The King of Tularosa," was a controversial character who dominated affairs around Tularosa into the 1880s, but then lost his grip (and property) due to lawsuits and defaults on loans. For a biography of Coghlan, see C. L. Sonnichsen, *Tularosa: Last of the Frontier West* (Albuquerque: University of New Mexico Press, 1980, 2nd ed.), 247–59.

Chapter 6

1. Temporal was about eight miles north of Tularosa, near where Rinconada Creek (Temporal Canyon) issues from the western side of the Sacramentos. For Siringo's version of how Coghlan's involvement with stolen cattle was uncovered, see Charles A. Siringo, *A Texas Cowboy* (New York: William Sloan Associates, 1950), 143–54. Siringo's account appeared in print in 1885 and he did not mention Meadows, who perhaps enhanced on his own role.

2. "Overland to California" and "Billy the Kid as I Knew Him," by John P. Meadows, in Philip J. Rasch files, Lincoln State Monument, Lincoln, N.Mex. Mr. Meadows continues his story

about the stolen Texas cattle in chapter 10. John W. Poe's version of this affair, in the April 22, 1882, issue of the *Santa Fe Daily New Mexican,* carries the story into April of 1882 and largely parallels Meadows's account, but does not mention either Meadows or Siringo. Robert Utley in his *Billy the Kid: A Short and Violent Life* (Lincoln: University of Nebraska Press, 1989), notes that Siringo indulged in a lifetime effort at self-glorification, and Meadows may have exaggerated his own part in retelling episodes from his life.

Chapter 7

1. The actual warrant, dated December 26, 1881, was returned by Sheriff Pat Garrett on May 8, 1882, and is reproduced in T. Dudley Cramer, *The Pecos Ranchers in the Lincoln County War* (Orinda, Calif.: Branding Iron Press, 1996), 154–55. Garrett certified that after using due diligence, the within-named Hugh M. Beckwith had not been found. Meadows's chronology is off by a year, since the events he described necessarily took place in the spring of 1882, not "the early spring of 1881." At the latter date, he and Tom Norris were farming on the Rio Peñasco (see chapter 3). Dudley Cramer cites Meadows's story as he told it to J. Evetts Haley in 1933; see Cramer, *The Pecos Ranchers,* 171–72.

2. Mack, or Mac, was a nickname. For a brief biography of McKittrick see James D. Shinkle, *Reminiscences of Roswell Pioneers* (Roswell: Hall-Poorbaugh Press, 1966), 85–87.

3. *Choza*—a cabin or hut; in this context clearly a dugout.

4. This incident happened on July 3, 1880, before Garrett became Lincoln County sheriff. See Philip J. Rasch, *Warriors of Lincoln County,* ed. Robert K. DeArment (Stillwater, Okla.: National Association for Outlaw and Lawman History, 1998), 126, 128.

5. *Alamogordo News,* Dec. 26, 1935, p. 1; "Overland to California," by John P. Meadows, in Philip J. Rasch files, Lincoln State Monument, Lincoln, N.Mex. For more details on Hugh Beckwith's tragic end, see Cramer, *The Pecos Ranchers,* 175–76.

Chapter 8

1. Tom Keeney, age forty-one, with wife, Isabel, and two daughters, was living in the La Luz precinct when enumerated June 4 in the 1880 Census. He gave his occupation as carpenter. NA, 10th Census (1880), Population Schedules, Enumeration District #13 page 14, Doña Ana County, N.Mex., T9 Roll 802.

2. Maruchi Canyon joins La Luz Canyon about five miles east of the community of La Luz.

3. *Alamogordo News,* Feb. 13, 1936, pp. 1, 4; "Overland to California," by John P. Meadows, in Philip J. Rasch files, Lincoln State Monument, Lincoln, N.Mex. As in chapter 7, Meadows's chronology puts the events in this story a year earlier than when they took place. The officer must have been 2nd Lieutenant George W. Van Deusen, 4th U.S. Cavalry. He was the only officer with a name similar to "Van Dusen" in the nineteenth-century army. Three companies of the 4th Cavalry were stationed at Fort Stanton from December 1881 into 1884, and in May 1882 they chased renegade Mescalero Apaches in the Sacramento and Guadalupe Mountains. See S. C. Agnew, *Garrisons of the Regular U.S. Army, New Mexico, 1846–1899* (Santa Fe, N.Mex.: Press of The Territorian, 1971), 52–53, and Lee Myers, *Fort Stanton, New Mexico, The Military Years 1855–1896* (Lincoln, N.Mex.: Lincoln County Historical Society, publication no. 2, 1993), 39.

Chapter 9

1. Phil Rasch wrote an account of this affair, "The Tularosa Ditch War," *New Mexico Historical Review* 43(3) (1968): 229–35.

2. A depression in the earth, in this case evidently flooded.

3. *Alamogordo News,* Oct. 10, Dec. 26, 1935; Jan. 16, 1936, all p. 1; "Billy the Kid as I Knew Him," by John P. Meadows, in Philip J. Rasch files, Lincoln State Monument, Lincoln, N.Mex.

Chapter 10

1. *Alamogordo News,* Aug. 15, Oct. 10, 1935, Jan. 16, 1936, all p. 1; "Billy the Kid as I Knew Him" and "Overland to

California," by John P. Meadows, in Philip J. Rasch files, Lincoln State Monument, Lincoln, N.Mex.

2. Meadows did well in keeping a complicated sequence of events reasonably straight. For a contemporary and more detailed account, see the *Santa Fe Daily New Mexican,* April 22, 1882; also Darlis A. Miller, *The California Column in New Mexico* (Albuquerque: University of New Mexico Press, 1982), 76–77. The case was carried over to the September term of court and two of the Texas Panhandle cattle companies won judgments against Coghlan; see C. L. Sonnichsen, *Tularosa: Last of the Frontier West* (Albuquerque: University of New Mexico Press, 1980, 2nd ed.), 254–55.

3. *Alamogordo News,* Aug. 15, 1935, p. 1; Meadows, "Billy the Kid as I Knew Him," in Rasch files. See also Philip J. Rasch, "The Nesmith Murder Mystery," *The Denver Westerners Monthly Roundup* 17(5) (1961): 16–20; and Miller, *California Column,* 77–78.

Although John Meadows says at one place that Nesmith was Coghlan's foreman, and again that he was manager of Pat Coghlan's Three Rivers farm at the time of his death (August 17, 1882, according to Sonnichsen, *Tularosa,* 255), Meadows also says that after court adjourned in the spring, Coghlan had no more use for either Meadows or the Nesmiths. From the information available it appears more likely that Coghlan had ceased to employ Nesmith, who was working as Meadows's partner at the latter's Three Rivers ranch or farm at the time of the Nesmith murders. Meadows does not tell us everything, and at this time (1882) he was using the name Gray.

4. This article is from the March 10, 1883, issue of the *Rio Grande Republican* and by reference to chapter 12 the information in it came from Meadows, when he was "sailing" under the pseudonym of Gray. The article appears to be consistent with Meadows's later reminiscence in that he only learned the names of the murderers when he worked for Pat Garrett in 1885.

5. Benjamin Davies, whom Meadows referred to in his reminiscence, owned the San Augustine ranch from 1875 to 1893; see K. D. Stoes, "The Story of the San Augustine Ranch," *The New Mexico Stockman* 22(3), 36, 60–61; 22(4), 30–34 (March,

April 1957). In Lincoln County War literature this is usually referred to as the Shedd Ranch, from the name of the previous owner. W. W. Cox purchased the property in 1893.

Chapter 11

1. *Alamogordo News,* April 2, 1936, p. 1. The best available guide to place name locations in this area is the U.S. Forest Service map of Lincoln National Forest, although many of the names used by Meadows have gone out of use.

Chapter 12

1. Benjamin is about eighty miles north of Abilene, Texas.

2. Meadows was mistaken in that Garrett killed Joe Briscoe, a young hunter who had been with him several months. Garrett's partner, Willis Skeleton Glenn, was absent at the time; see Leon C. Metz, *Pat Garrett: The Story of a Western Lawman* (Norman: University of Oklahoma Press, 1974), 15–16.

3. *Alamogordo News,* March 8, 1936, pp. 1, 4.

4. C. L. Sonnichsen, *Tularosa: Last of the Frontier West* (Albuquerque: University of New Mexico Press, 1980, 2nd ed.), 26–27, 32–36, tells about the difficulties between McDonald and Good that ended with McDonald's murder in June 1888. No one was charged or tried.

5. *Alamogordo News,* March 12, 1936, p. 1. Sonnichsen expands a bit on the association of Garrett and Meadows with the Angus VV Ranch in 1885 in *Tularosa,* 235. Pat Garrett and his family didn't leave for Uvalde until 1891 (Metz, *Pat Garrett,* 127).

Chapter 13

1. Johnson fell through the trap on November 19, 1886; see John P. Wilson, *Merchants, Guns, and Money: The Story of Lincoln County and Its Wars* (Santa Fe: Museum of New Mexico Press, 1987), 151.

2. *Alamogordo News,* Aug. 8, 1935, p. 1.

Chapter 14

1. This story, "about which I told you," evidently was not printed by the *Alamogordo News.*
2. *Alamogordo News,* Jan. 2, 1936, p. 1.

Chapter 15

1. Also spelled Natsile, Nautzile, and Notzili; see C. L. Sonnichsen, *The Mescalero Apaches* (Norman: University of Oklahoma Press, 1958), 153, 157, opp. p. 165, 172, 178, 213, 218.
2. Agent Rhodes dated this affair to February 3, 1892, and passed over it quickly in his annual report; see *Sixty-First Annual Report of the Commissioner of Indian Affairs . . . 1892* (Washington, D.C.: Government Printing Office, 1892), 330. Sonnichsen, *The Mescalero Apaches,* 220, obviously relied upon Meadows almost entirely for his information.
3. *Alamogordo News,* Feb. 20, 1936, p. 1.
4. The marriage certificate for Miss Callie Sikes and Walter Trimble is on file in Lincoln County Transcripts, vol. A, Misc. Contracts and Agreements, page 47, at Otero County Clerk's office, Alamogordo, N.Mex. Minister J. C. *Gage* (not George) married them on December 22, 1892, at Weed, N.Mex.
5. P. I. & I. Co. was the Pecos Irrigation and Improvement Company, formed July 1, 1890, to take over the assets and assume the liabilities of two former investment and irrigation companies.
6. The bank would have been the First National Bank of Eddy, Chas. B. Eddy, president, H. P. Brown, cashier, which had advertised in the *Eddy Argus,* October 3, 1891 (see Lee Myers, *The Pearl of the Pecos* [Carlsbad, N.Mex.: Privately printed, 1974], 60). There was a lot more to this story. According to Dee Harkey, Harry Brown ran off with about $12,000 from the bank plus another $16,000 he had stolen while serving as Eddy County Treasurer. Harkey, evidently working as a bounty hunter, pursued the accused first to Chihuahua, then to El Paso, Chicago, Terre Haute, and finally to Cripple Creek, Colorado. Returned to Eddy County, Brown was sentenced to the penitentiary, but the

territorial governor pardoned him the day he arrived (Dee Harkey, *Mean as Hell* (Albuquerque: University of New Mexico Press, 1948), 73–76.

7. Uvalde has been a major agricultural area for more than a century but the water comes from pumping groundwater. No mention of a proposed "big dam and irrigation works" is found in Ron Tyler, editor-in-chief, *The New Handbook of Texas*, vols. 1–6 (Austin: The Texas State Historical Association, 1996); in Paul S. Taylor's *An American-Mexican Frontier: Nueces County, Texas* (New York: Russell & Russell, 1971); or in the Nueces County Historical Society's *The History of Nueces County* (Austin: Jenkins Book Publishing Co., 1972).

8. *Alamogordo News*, Feb. 27, 1936, pp. 1–2. Meadows's account of events at Fort Stockton leaves much unsaid and includes some errors. The Leon Water Holes, or Leon Springs, were about seven miles west, not east, of Fort Stockton. In 1889 A. J. (Andy) Royal acquired a large irrigated farm there that he worked, apparently by sharecropping, with tenants.

Royal, elected sheriff of Pecos County in November 1892, had killed a man earlier that year but was not indicted. He was also suspected in the thefts of many horses that summer. In 1893–1894, he was indicted for several unprovoked assaults, which were remaining to be heard when a new sheriff was sworn in on Nov. 12, 1894. Meadows and others had been charged with assisting a prisoner to escape, but evidently the justice of the peace at Del Rio released them. Meadows wisely left. On the afternoon of Nov. 21, Andy Royal was assassinated by a blast from a shotgun while sitting in a chair in the sheriff's office. No one saw who did it. For these and other details, see Bill C. James and Mary Kay Shannon, *Sheriff A. J. Royal: Fort Stockton, Texas* (n.p., 1984).

Chapter 16

1. The Taylor Grazing Act became effective in 1936, even as Meadows was talking with the reporter. This act established grazing districts and required payment for grazing permits on the public domain for the first time; see U.S. Bureau of Land Management, *Historical Highlights of Public Land*

Management (Washington, D.C.: Government Printing Office, 1962), 53, 55.

2. The Hilton ranch was the predecessor of the Circle Cross ranch. The "headquarters" lay on the Sacramento River just above Timberon, N.Mex.

3. In another internal inconsistency, the chronology given here obviously conflicts with the one in the previous chapter.

4. *Alamogordo News,* April 9, 1936, pp. 1, 2; also February 13, 1947, p. 1. Sonnichsen summarized this episode in *Tularosa: Last of the Frontier West* (Albuquerque: University of New Mexico Press, 1980, 2nd ed.), 87–89, partly from Meadows's account.

Chapter 17

1. The W. N. Fleck home ranch was four miles east of the railroad depot at Orogrande, N.Mex.; see Meinzer and Hare, *Geology and Water Resources of Tularosa Basin, New Mexico,* USGS Water Supply Paper 343 (Washington, D.C.: Government Printing Office, 1915), 253. That study and the U.S. Geological Survey's Point of Sands and Tularosa N.Mex. 30' quad maps (both 1916) are the best available early maps of the Tularosa Basin, but are too recent to show many of Meadows's place names.

2. *Alamogordo News,* March 26, 1936, p. 1.

Chapter 18

1. This letter by Meadows to the *Doña Ana County Republican,* March 11, 1897, p.1, is the only contemporary letter by him that has been found. It documents his service as a deputy for Sheriff Pat Garrett at the time and that Garrett was not inactive in searching for evidence of the murders of Colonel Albert J. Fountain and his son during 1896–1897. Meadows chose not to mention his involvement in the investigation of Fountain's apparent death in any of his stories. The same issue of this March 11th paper noted that "Deputy Sheriff Meadows returned from Rincon yesterday" and "Deputy Sheriff Meadows left for the Organs today to summon some jurors."

Chapter 19

1. Paraje, which no longer exists, was a small community on the east side of the Rio Grande where the Camino Real turned away from the river to continue south across the Jornada del Muerto. The town lay about where the head of Elephant Butte Reservoir normally reaches.

2. *Alamogordo News,* March 19, 1936, p. 1. John Meadows was entirely wrong in his last two paragraphs, about Rito's career in crime following his escape on Pat Garrett's racehorse. In September 1898 he murdered a man at San Marcial in Socorro County and fled to Arizona. Arrested and held in Willcox, Sheriff Pat Garrett returned him to New Mexico, where he pled guilty to second-degree murder and was sentenced to the penitentiary for life. He arrived there on December 21, 1899.

Rito, now convict no. 1281, had an accident at the prison almost three years later. While working alone on the second floor of the brick plant, he fell into the brick-making machinery and was crushed to death by one of the heavy cog wheels. This was the first accident of any kind since the brick plant had been installed.

At the time of his capture in 1899, his popular image was definitely suffering. One Las Cruces paper labeled Rito "one of the most desperate and cold blooded criminals that ever went unhung" (see *Dona Ana County Republican,* September 28, 1899, p. 1 and December 9, 1899, p. 4; *Santa Fe New Mexican* November 22, 1902, p. 1 and November 24, 1902, p. 4; New Mexico State Records Center and Archives, N.Mex. Department of Corrections records, Penitentiary of New Mexico, Convict Description Book 1884–1912, Reel No. 1, p. 86).

Epilogue

1. Robert M. Utley, *Billy the Kid: A Short and Violent Life* (Lincoln: University of Nebraska Press, 1989), 264 endnote 15.

2. *Las Vegas Morning Gazette,* June 16, 1881 (extracts in Phil Rasch files). *Las Vegas Daily Optic,* May 14, 1881, p. 4 said that when Barney Mason and Jim Cureton met the Kid, Barney took to his heels while Cureton rode up and talked with him.

3. *Las Vegas Daily Optic,* May 10, 1881, p. 1; Utley, *Billy the Kid,* 186–87, 265–66; Frederick Nolan, *The West of Billy the Kid* (Norman: University of Oklahoma Press, 1998), 276–77; Elvis E. Fleming, *J. B. 'Billy' Mathews: Biography of a Lincoln County Deputy* (Las Cruces, N.Mex.: Yucca Tree Press, 1999), 50–51.

4. Utley, *Billy the Kid,* 133–34; Nolan, *West of Billy the Kid,* 239; Donald Cline, *Alias Billy the Kid: The Man Behind the Legend* (Santa Fe, N.Mex.: Sunstone Press, 1986), 88–89.

5. Newspapers examined closely for this period include the Las Cruces *Thirty-Four, The Advance* (Albuquerque), and *The Grant County Herald* (Silver City), for which nearly complete runs survive. Holdings of *Las Vegas Daily Optic* and *The Albuquerque Review* are more scattered, while issues of *The Mesilla News* are nearly nonexistent for 1880. The first newspapers in White Oaks and Socorro appeared later in 1880.

6. Susan E. Wallace, *The Land of the Pueblos* (New York: John B. Alden, 1889), 156; *The Mesilla News,* Jan. 29, 1881, p. 2; Joseph A. Stout Jr., *Apache Lightning: The Last Great Battles of the Ojo Calientes* Ojo Calientes (New York: Oxford University Press, 1974), 145.

7. *The Grant County Herald,* May 29, 1880, p. 2; Stout, *Apache Lightning,* 137; Dan L. Thrapp, *The Conquest of Apacheria* (Norman: University of Oklahoma Press, 1967), 198.

8. Richard N. Ellis, editor, "'The Apache Chronicle'," *New Mexico Historical Review* 47(3) (1972): 275–82. Stout, *Apache Lightning,* 134–52.

9. *The Grant County Herald,* Feb. 21, 1880, pp. 1, 2.

10. *The Advance,* April 8, 1880, p. 1; *The Albuquerque Review,* April 10, 1880, p. 2; *Thirty-Four,* April 21, 1880, p. 3.

11. *Thirty-Four,* April 28, 1880, p. 1, and *The Advance,* May 1 and 22, 1880, both p. 3; Joseph P. Peters, *Indian Battles and Skirmishes on the American Frontier, 1790–1898* (New York: Argonaut Press Ltd., 1966), 49. Rinconada Canyon runs south and west from the Sierra Blanca while Carrizosa referred to the ranch just north of modern Carrizozo, N.Mex.

12. Utley, *Billy the Kid,* 21–25; Nolan, *West of Billy the Kid,* 68–69, 76–79; Robert N. Mullin, editor, *Maurice Garland*

Fulton's History of the Lincoln County War (Tucson: The University of Arizona Press, 1968), 68–69.

13. Cline, *Alias Billy the Kid,* 55; William A. Keleher, *Violence in Lincoln County, 1869–1881: A New Mexico Item* (Albuquerque: University of New Mexico Press, 1957), 311–12; Jerry Weddle, *Antrim is My Stepfather's Name: The Boyhood of Billy the Kid* (Tucson: The Arizona Historical Society, 1993), 44–47, 66–67.

14. Pat F. Garrett, *The Authentic Life of Billy, the Kid* (Norman: University of Oklahoma Press, 1954), 31.

15. *The Mesilla News,* July 3, 1875, p. 3; *The Mesilla Valley Independent,* Sept. 15, 1877, p. 3; *Thirty-Four,* May 19, 1880, p. 3; *Rio Grande Republican,* June 4, 1881, p. 2; New Mexico State Records Center and Archives (NMSRCA), Territorial Archives of New Mexico, reel 50, frames 217, 223–25, 297.

16. NMSRCA, Territorial Archives of New Mexico, reel 50, frames 278–79.

17. Cline, *Alias Billy the Kid,* 55–57.

18. Mullin, *Maurice Garland Fulton's History,* 393–34.

19. *Philadelphia Times* (daily), July 20, 1881, p. 1; Philip J. Rasch, *Trailing Billy the Kid,* ed. Robert K. DeArment (National Association for Outlaw and Lawman History, Inc., 1995), 177; John P. Wilson, "Did you know Billy the Kid was his own press agent?" *Arizona Senior World,* May 1999, p. 57.

20. John P. Wilson, "With His Boots Off: First Newspaper Reports on the Death of Billy the Kid," *Rio Grande History,* no. 14 (1983): 11–13, 23.

21. Rasch, *Trailing Billy the Kid,* 29.

22. *Roswell Daily Record,* March 2, 1931, p. 6.

23. *Roswell Daily Record,* March 3, 1931, p. 6; Rasch, *Trailing Billy the Kid,* 65–68.

24. John P. Wilson, *When The Texans Came: Missing Records from the Civil War in the Southwest, 1861-1862* (Albuquerque: University of New Mexico Press, 2001), 7–8.

25. *Otero County Advertiser,* June 15, 1907, p. 4; *Tularosa Valley Tribune,* April 18, 1914, p. 8.

26. Nolan, *West of Billy the Kid,* 271–73, 324 note 12; Rasch, *Trailing Billy the Kid,* 135–36, 142; Utley, *Billy the Kid,* 179–81,

186–87, 202–3, 261–65; Leon C. Metz, *Pat Garrett: The Story of a Western Lawman* (Norman: University of Oklahoma Press, 1974), 15; C. L. Sonnichsen, *The Mescalero Apaches* (Norman: University of Oklahoma Press, 1958), 128, 190–91, 220; Sonnichsen, *Tularosa: Last of the Frontier West* (Albuquerque: University of New Mexico Press, 1980), 88–89, 303, 319; John P. Wilson, *Merchants, Guns, and Money: The Story of Lincoln County and Its Wars* (Santa Fe: Museum of New Mexico Press, 1987), 89.

27. Reprinted in Don Hampton Biggers, *Buffalo Guns & Barbed Wire: Two Frontier Accounts by Don Hampton Biggers* (Lubbock: Texas Tech University Press, 1991).

28. John P. Wilson, *Islands in the Desert: A History of the Uplands of Southeastern Arizona* (Albuquerque: University of New Mexico Press, 1995), 228.

References

Publications

Agnew, S. C. 1971. *Garrisons of the Regular U.S. Army, New Mexico, 1846–1899.* Santa Fe: The Press of The Territorian.

Bandelier, Adolph F. 1892. *Final Report of Investigations Among the Indians of the Southwestern United States, Carried on Mainly in the Years from 1880 to 1885,* part 2. Cambridge, Mass.: John Wilson and Son.

Biggers, Don Hampton. 1991. *Buffalo Guns and Barbed Wire: Two Frontier Accounts: A Combined Reissue of Pictures of the Past and History That Will Never Be Repeated.* Lubbock: Texas Tech University Press.

Burroughs, Jean M. 1980. *On the Trail: The Life and Tales of "Lead Steer" Potter.* Santa Fe: Museum of New Mexico Press.

Chávez, Tibo. 1978. "Colonel José Francisco Chávez, 1833–1904." *Rio Grande History,* no. 8: 6–9.

Cleaveland, Agnes Morley. 1941. *No Life for a Lady.* Boston: Houghton Mifflin Co.

Cline, Donald. 1986. *Alias Billy the Kid: The Man Behind the Legend.* Santa Fe, N.Mex.: Sunstone Press.

Coan, Charles F. 1925. *A History of New Mexico,* volume 3. Chicago and New York: The American Historical Society, Inc.

Cramer, T. Dudley. 1996. *The Pecos Ranchers in the Lincoln County War.* Orinda, Calif.: Branding Iron Press.

Ellis, Richard N., editor. 1972. "'The Apache Chronicle.'" *New Mexico Historical Review* 47(3): 275–82.

Fleming, Elvis E. 1999 *J. B. 'Billy' Mathews: Biography of a Lincoln County Deputy.* Las Cruces, N.Mex.: Yucca Tree Press.

————. 2002 *Captain Joseph C. Lea: From Confederate Guerrilla to New Mexico Patriarch.* Las Cruces, N.Mex.: Yucca Tree Press.

Garrett, Pat F. 1954 *The Authentic Life of Billy, the Kid.* With Introduction by Jeff C. Dykes. Norman: University of Oklahoma Press.

Gibson, A. M. 1965. *The Life and Death of Colonel Albert Jennings Fountain.* Norman: University of Oklahoma Press.

Harkey, Dee. 1948 *Mean as Hell.* Albuquerque: University of New Mexico Press.

Hill, Robert K., Jr.. 1983 "Settlement of the Southern Sacramentos, 1880 to 1912: Weed, Avis, Pinon, and Environs." *The Greater Llano Estacado Southwest Heritage* 13(2): 14–22.

Hunt, Frazier. 1956. *The Tragic Days of Billy the Kid.* New York: Hastings House.

James, Bill C., and Mary Kay Shannon. 1984. *Sheriff A. J. Royal: Fort Stockton, Texas.* N.p.

Keleher, William A. 1957. *Violence in Lincoln County, 1869–1881; A New Mexico Item.* Albuquerque, University of New Mexico Press.

————. 1962. *The Fabulous Frontier; Twelve New Mexico Items,* revised edition. Albuquerque: University of New Mexico Press.

Larson, Carole. 1993. *Forgotten Frontier: The Story of Southeastern New Mexico.* Albuquerque: University of New Mexico Press.

Meinzer, O. E., and R. F. Hare. 1915. *Geology and Water Resources of Tularosa Basin, New Mexico.* U.S. Geological Survey Water Supply Paper 343. Washington, D.C.: Government Printing Office.

Metz, Leon C. 1974. *Pat Garrett: The Story of a Western Lawman.* Norman: University of Oklahoma Press.

————. 1980. *John Selman, Gunfighter,* second edition. Norman: University of Oklahoma Press.

Miller, Darlis A. 1982. *The California Column in New Mexico.* Albuquerque: University of New Mexico Press.

Morrison, Charles C. 1878. "Executive and Descriptive Report of Lieutenant Charles C. Morrison, Sixth Cavalry, on the Operations of Party No. 2, Colorado Section, Field Season of 1877" [Wheeler Survey], Appendix F to Appendix NN of *Annual Report of the Chief of Engineers for 1878* (Serial Set #1846). Washington, D.C.: Government Printing Office.

Mullin, Robert N., editor. 1968. *Maurice Garland Fulton's History of the Lincoln County War.* Tucson: The University of Arizona Press.

Myers, Lee. 1965. "Courage of Robert and Lucy Gilbert." *The West,* September 1965: 10–11, 54–56.

———. 1974. *The Pearl of the Pecos.* Carlsbad, N.Mex.: Privately printed.

———. 1993. *Fort Stanton, New Mexico, The Military Years 1855–1896.* Lincoln, N.Mex.: Lincoln County Historical Society, Publication no. 2.

Nolan, Frederick. 1992. *The Lincoln County War: A Documentary History.* Norman: University of Oklahoma Press.

———. 1998. *The West of Billy the Kid.* Norman: University of Oklahoma Press.

Nueces County Historical Society. 1972. *The History of Nueces County.* Austin: Jenkins Book Publishing Co.

Owen, Gordon R. 1996. *The Two Alberts: Fountain and Fall.* Las Cruces, N.Mex.: Yucca Tree Press.

Peters, Joseph P. 1966. *Indian Battles and Skirmishes on the American Frontier, 1790–1898.* New York: Argonaut Press Ltd.

Rasch, Philip J. 1956. "The Horrell War." *New Mexico Historical Review* 31(3): 223–31.

———. 1961. "The Nesmith Murder Mystery." *The Denver Westerners Monthly Roundup* 17(5): 16–20.

———. 1968. "The Tularosa Ditch War." *New Mexico Historical Review* 43(3): 229–35.

———. 1995. *Trailing Billy the Kid.* Edited by Robert K. DeArment. Laramie, Wyo.: National Association for Outlaw and Lawman History, Inc.

———. 1998. *Warriors of Lincoln County.* Edited by Robert
K. DeArment. Stillwater, Okla.: National Association for
Outlaw and Lawman History.

Shinkle, James D. 1966. *Reminiscences of Roswell Pioneers.*
Roswell, N.Mex.: Hall-Poorbaugh Press.

Smith, Robert Kermit, Jr. 1985. "Sacramento Mountain
Pioneers." *The Greater Llano Estacado Southwest
Heritage* 14(1): 1–4, 18–20.

Siringo, Charles A. 1950. *A Texas Cowboy.* New York: William
Sloan Associates.

———. 1975. *The Song Companion of a Lone Star Cowboy:
Old Favorite Cow-Camp Songs.* Reprint of 1919 edition.
Norwood, Pa.: Norwood editions.

Sonnichsen, C. L. 1958. *The Mescalero Apaches.* Norman:
University of Oklahoma Press.

———. 1980. *Tularosa: Last of the Frontier West,* second edition. Albuquerque: University of New Mexico Press.

Southeastern New Mexico Historical Society. 1982. *Eddy
County New Mexico to 1981.* Carlsbad, N.Mex.:
Southeastern New Mexico Historical Society.

Stoes, K. D. 1957. "The Story of the San Augustine Ranch." *The
New Mexico Stockman* 22(3): 36, 60–61; 22(4): 30–34.

Stout, Joseph A., Jr. 1974. *Apache Lightning: The Last Great
Battles of the Ojo Calientes.* New York: Oxford University
Press.

Taylor, Paul S. 1971. *An American-Mexican Frontier: Nueces
County, Texas.* New York: Russell & Russell.

Thompson, Jerry, editor. 1990. "With the Third Infantry in New
Mexico, 1851–1853; The Lost Diary of Private Sylvester W.
Matson." *The Journal of Arizona History* 31(4): 349–404.

Thrapp, Dan L. 1967. *The Conquest of Apacheria.* Norman:
University of Oklahoma Press.

———. 1974. *Victorio and the Mimbres Apaches.* Norman:
University of Oklahoma Press.

Tyler, Ron, editor-in-chief. 1996. *The New Handbook of Texas,*
vols. 1–6. Austin: The Texas State Historical Association.

U.S. Bureau of Land Management. 1962. *Historical Highlights
of Public Land Management.* Washington, D.C.:

Government Printing Office.

U.S. Commissioner of Indian Affairs. 1892. *Sixty-First Annual Report of the Commissioner of Indian Affairs . . . 1892.* Washington, D.C.: Government Printing Office.

Utley, Robert M. 1989. *Billy the Kid: A Short and Violent Life.* Lincoln: University of Nebraska Press.

Wallace, Susan E. 1889. *The Land of the Pueblos.* New York: John B. Alden, Publisher.

Weddle, Jerry. 1993. *Antrim is My Stepfather's Name: The Boyhood of Billy the Kid.* Historical Monograph no. 9. Tucson: The Arizona Historical Society.

Wilson, John P. 1983. "With His Boots Off: First Newspaper Reports on the Death of Billy the Kid." *Rio Grande History,* no. 14: 11–13, 23.

———. 1987. *Merchants, Guns, and Money: The Story of Lincoln County and Its Wars.* Santa Fe: Museum of New Mexico Press.

———. 1995. *Islands in the Desert: A History of the Uplands of Southeastern Arizona.* Albuquerque: University of New Mexico Press.

———. 1999. "Did you know Billy the Kid was his own press agent?" *Arizona Senior World,* May 1999, p. 57. Tempe, Arizona.

———. 2001. *When the Texans Came: Missing Records from the Civil War in the Southwest, 1861–1862.* Albuquerque: University of New Mexico Press.

Manuscripts, Microfilms, and Websites

Lincoln State Monument, Lincoln, New Mexico. "Cowboy in Texas," "Overland to California," and "Billy the Kid as I Knew Him," by John P. Meadows, 78 pp. manuscript in Philip J. Rasch files.

National Archives and Records Administration, Washington, D.C., RG 29, Records of the Bureau of the Census. 10th Census (1880), Population Schedules, Enumeration District #13, Doña Ana County; Precinct #5, Lincoln

County; Precinct #22 and Enumeration District #37 (Sunnyside and Fort Sumner), San Miguel County, N.Mex., Microfilm Publication T9 Rolls 802, 803.

———. 12th Census (1900), Population Schedules, Precinct #3, Otero County, N.Mex., Microfilm Publication T623 Roll 1001.

———. 13th Census (1910), Population Schedules, Precinct #2, Otero County, N.Mex., Microfilm Publication T624 Roll 916.

———. 14th Census (1920), Population Schedules, Precinct #3, Otero County, N.Mex., Microfilm Publication T625 Roll 1077.

National Archives and Records Administration, Washington, D.C., RG 393, Records of U.S. Army Continental Commands, 1821–1920. Letters Sent by the 9th Military Department, the Department of New Mexico, and the District of New Mexico, 1849–1890, Microfilm Publication M-1072:

Roll 6, Name and Subject Indices to Vols. 18–20 (in part), 1878–1881, and vols. 18–20.

Roll 7, Name and Subject Indices to Vols. 20 (in part)–23, 1881–1890, and vols. 21–23.

———. Registers of Letters Received by Headquarters, District of New Mexico, Sept. 1865–Aug. 1890, Microfilm Publication M-1097:

Roll 6, Indices and Vols. 13–14, Jan. 4, 1879–May 12, 1881.

———. Register of Letters Received and Letters Received by Headquarters, 9th Military Department, 1848–1853, Microfilm Publication M-1102:

Roll 5, 1852 D-S.

New Mexico State Records Center and Archives, Santa Fe, N.Mex. Archdiocese of Santa Fe, Santa Rita Parish, Carrizozo, N.Mex. Marriages, 1869–1956, "Registro de los Casamientos del Condado de Lincoln, desde 1869–1903" (microfilm).

———. Department of Corrections records, Penitentiary of New Mexico, Convict Description Book 1884–1912, Reel no. 1.

Territorial Archives of New Mexico, Microfilm edition, reel 41, Territorial Census of 1885, Lincoln–San Miguel counties; reel 50, Records of the Territorial Auditor, Doña Ana County, Nov. 7, 1853–June 30, 1897.

Otero County Clerk's Office, Alamogordo, N.Mex. Bound volumes:
Deed Records, Books 11, 13, 17, 47, 49, 78, 81, 102.
Lincoln County Transcripts, Vol. A, Miscellaneous Contracts and Agreements.
Liquor, Occupation and Gambling Licenses, 1899–1979.
Marriages, Book 1.
Miscellaneous, Books 40, 97.
Mortgage Deeds, Book 100.
Probate File #533 (estate of Mary E. Meadows).
Quit Claim Deeds, Book 79.
Release Records, Book 81.
Tax Deeds, Book 113.
Will Book 1 (Mary E. Meadows).
Village of Tularosa, N.Mex. Minute Book (#2), Board of Trustees of the Village of Tularosa, April 6, 1926, to Dec. 2, 1936.

Website for 5th Georgia Infantry Regiment CSA at: http://www.researchonline.net/gacw/unit21.htm.

Newspapers

The Advance (Albuquerque, N.Mex.). April 8, May 1, 22, 1880.
Alamogordo Advertiser (Alamogordo, N.Mex.). Feb. 2, 1933; June 25, 1936.
Alamogordo News (Alamogordo, N.Mex.). June 28, 1900; Feb. 2, 16, 1933; Aug. 8, 15, 1935; Sept. 5, 12, 26, 1935; Oct. 3, 10, 17, 24, 31, 1935; Nov. 14, 21, 28, 1935; Dec. 1, 5, 12, 19, 26, 1935; Jan. 2, 9, 16, 23, 30, 1936; Feb. 6, 13, 20, 27, 1936; March 8, 12, 19, 26, 1936; April 2, 9, 16, 1936; May 7, 14, 21, 1936; June 11, 25, 1936; Feb. 13, 1947.

The Albuquerque Review (Albuquerque, N.Mex.). April 10, 1880.

Doña Ana County Republican (Las Cruces, N.Mex.). March 11, April 1, 1897; Sept. 28, Dec. 9, 1899.

The Golden Era (Lincoln, N.Mex.). Aug 6, Nov. 5, 1885.

The Grant County Herald (Silver City, N.Mex.). Feb. 21, May 29, Sept. 11, 18, 1880.

Independent Democrat (Las Cruces, N.Mex.). March 25, 1896; March 30, 1898.

Las Vegas Daily Optic (Las Vegas, N.Mex.). Jan. 21, May 10, 14, 1881.

Las Vegas Morning Gazette (Las Vegas, N.Mex.). June 16, 1881.

The Mesilla News (Mesilla, N.Mex.). July 3, 1875; Sept. 18, 1880; Jan. 29, 1881.

The Mesilla Valley Independent (Mesilla, N.Mex.). Sept. 15, 1877.

Otero County Advertiser (Alamogordo, N.Mex.). June 15, 1907.

Philadelphia Times (daily; Philadelphia, Pa.). July 20, 1881.

Rio Grande Republican (Las Cruces, N.Mex.). June 4, 1881; March 10, 1883; April 8, 15, 22, May 20, July 8, Dec. 23, 1898; April 12, June 2, 9, 16, 1899.

Roswell Daily Record (Roswell, N.Mex.). Feb. 17, 20, 26, 27, March 2, 3, 4, 1931.

Santa Fe Daily New Mexican (Santa Fe, N.Mex.). April 22, 1882.

Santa Fe New Mexican (Santa Fe, N.Mex.). Nov. 22, 24, 1902.

Thirty-Four (Las Cruces, N.Mex.). Oct. 15, 22, 1879; April 21, 28, May 5, 19, Sept. 8, 15, 29, 1880.

The Tularosa Democrat (Tularosa, N.Mex.). Jan. 7, Feb. 25, 1904.

Tularosa Valley Tribune (Tularosa, N.Mex.). April 18, June 27, 1914; April 22, 29, Oct. 7, 1916.

Personal Communications

Mr. George Abbott, Alamogordo, N.Mex., 1996.

Mrs. Jo Anderson, Alamogordo, N.Mex., 1996.

Mr. Jim Bradshaw, J. Evetts Haley History Center, Midland, Texas, Feb. 4, 2002.

Chaves County Clerk's office, Roswell, N.Mex., Jan. 15, 2002.

Mrs. Norma Cinert, Tularosa, N.Mex., 1996, 2003.

Eddy County Clerk's office, Carlsbad, N.Mex., c. Jan. 30, 2002.

Michael F. Knight, National Archives (Washington D.C.), Oct. 7, 2002.

Mrs. Loraine Lavender, Santa Fe, N.Mex., c. 1983–1986.

Mrs. Lucille Marr, Tularosa, N.Mex., 1996.

Mrs. Christine Myers, Las Cruces, N.Mex., July 29, 2003.

New Mexico Bureau of Vital Records, Santa Fe, N.Mex., August 7, 1996.

St. Francis de Paula Parish registry office, Tularosa, N.Mex., May 15, 2001.

Index